Primary Plants

Q

QUESTIONS
PUBLISHING

Primary Plants

A handbook for teaching plant science in the primary school

Martin Braund

THE QUESTIONS PUBLISHING COMPANY LTD

BIRMINGHAM

2001

The Questions Publishing Company Ltd
27 Frederick Street, Birmingham B1 3HH

First published in 2001

ISBN: 1-84190-038-9
Illustrations by Felicity House, Graham-Cameron Illustration
Cover design by Al Stewart

Printed in the UK

Contents

List of copiable worksheets

Introduction

Why teach children about plants?

The National Curriculum says we have to – but there must be more to it than this. Work with plants, particularly on growth, has been a popular topic in primary schools for some time. Yet research shows that children know far less about plants than they do about animals. By the time they get to secondary school children think plants are boring. If this carries on, few will go on to provide us with the plant scientists we need in the future. These are sound educational reasons for this book, but there are others.

Plants are fascinating. Without them none of us would be here. Humans have depended on them in one way or another throughout history. It may seem surprising in this technologically advanced world, but we are now more dependant on plants than stone age people were. Every day we wash and preen ourselves with plant products, feed on them, wear them, travel on them, use them when we are ill and, ultimately, when we die. Plants are big business. The challenge to produce more food at lower cost has spawned a whole batch of new plant technologies – some of which, like genetic modification of crops, are controversial.

In the age of TV makeover, plants are stars. Gardening programmes are hugely popular and their presenters attract cult status. Garden centres and supermarkets overflow with a bewildering range of plant produce to grow and eat. Their tills overflow, too, if the queues on a spring bank holiday are anything to go by.

Plants have always dominated our culture. It is said that one thousand years ago a squirrel could have travelled the length and breadth of the country without putting a foot on the ground, such was the completeness of Britain's woodland carpet. In the ancient world, tree magic and woodland spirits ruled. Some of the old traditions survive. We still 'deck the halls' of our houses with greenery, originally used to appease woodland gods, at the pagan midwinter drinking feast we now call Christmas. Many other cultures and religions celebrate and worship with plants, and this is an example of diversity in multicultural Britain.

Plants are powerful symbols. Every country in the British Isles has a flower as its emblem. We give roses to show love and keep clover and heather for luck. Poppies used on Armistice Day are reminders of ones that sprouted from first world war fields of battle in which so many young people died. Trees hold special significance for many people. They are planted as memorials, and individual trees like the General

Oak of Sherwood Forest, that supposedly hid Robin Hood, are famous. When large numbers of trees are lost, as in the devastating hurricane in England in 1987 and the French storms of late 1999, there is a distinct sense of public loss.

In today's age of pre-packed, ready-made, off-the-shelf, on-line produce, children are increasingly isolated from the natural scheme of things. *Primary Plants* is the resource that helps put children in touch with this world, and plant science back in the front line of science education.

What this book contains

Primary Plants has been written so that schools, teachers and children can reach into the world of plants and be more informed about them. This book represents a complete guide to teaching about plants.

Each chapter focuses on one main concept area. To help with planning, links with the National Curriculum (2000 version), and the national scheme of work for science, published by the Qualifications and Curriculum Authority (QCA), have been made clear at the start of each chapter. A summary of these links and associated key ideas is provided on page 150.

Each chapter includes enough detail to give the teacher confidence in her or his understanding of the background science. The information also provides sources for stories and anecdotes about plants and their uses that will enrich your lessons.

We know quite a lot about the difficulties that children have in learning about plants, so the common misconceptions that might cause problems are shown for guidance.

The introduction of literacy and numeracy strategies has put a squeeze on curriculum time for science, so teachers need ways in which science can feed into english and mathematics lessons. An extensive list of suggestions for linking plant work to literacy and numeracy in Key Stages 1 and 2 is included for each concept area. Ideas for using information and communication technology (ICT) to teach about plant science is also included. A list of resources, including websites, features at the end of the book.

A chapter on festivals and celebrations using plants has been included so that cultural diversity and tradition can be featured. This chapter supports new curriculum guidelines for promoting learning across the curriculum, including the new framework for PSHE (personal, social and health education).

Learning activities

Plenty of ideas for activities are provided in each chapter. These are clearly linked with the appropriate key stage.

Activities to support work in literacy and numeracy are linked to objectives for National Curriculum year groups in line with the national strategy documents. You will find a vocabulary list for each area of teaching clearly linked to key stages. The suggestions for ICT are linked with the QCA scheme of work now used by many schools.

Varied and stimulating practical work abounds and extensive use has been made of new ideas in teaching, for example, techniques promoted by the Science and Plants for Schools project (SAPS). Each chapter includes copiable sheets that can be used to support practical work.

A major issue in primary science is how to ensure progression, particularly in investigative work. Teachers and science coordinators can sometimes find this difficult to cope with. The last chapter uses a 'flowerpot' model to show how progression works. This could form the basis of Inset work in school, as the model works for any area of scientific enquiry.

The resources section gives details of books, learning packs, Internet sites and places of interest that can be used to enhance learning about plants. Examples of fiction, poems and non-fiction are included to help teachers plan and resource literacy work, and for use in the school library.

Plant pictures – using the CD-ROM

Images of plants and the ways they are used are provided on a CD-ROM for teachers and children to use in a number of ways. The full-colour images relate to many of the themes and ideas featured in this book. A complete list of photographs included on the CD-ROM can be found at the end of this book.

Many of the photographs in this book are included on the CD-ROM.

Use the CD-ROM:

- for children to select, cut and paste images of plants and plant structures into their own work;
- for the teacher to show images to the whole class using a computer;
- to provide images that can be included in teacher written classroom materials;

- as a resource loaded onto a server, internal school network and/ or website, so it is accessible to all teachers and children in the school, as well as an outside audience, including parents;
- as images that can be set in screensavers, multimedia presentations and scrolling slide-shows;
- as sources·for cross-curricular work including art and PSHE;
- as images to stimulate discussion, e.g. by asking children what images might mean to them, what questions the images raise, or what further things they might want to know.

Instructions on how to load and operate the CD-ROM can be found in Appendix 2.

Chapter 1

Our world of plants

IF YOU ask children to come up with a list of plant products they have used in a day, you might get things like cornflakes, a table, maybe the paper they are writing on. But how many would include toothpaste, or even the toothbrush itself?

It is quite amazing how many everyday products come directly from plants or chemicals extracted from them. It's a story from life until death – from the drugs and fabrics used in the delivery room to the choice of wood for your coffin. To start with, let's look at some familiar categories of plant products.

Food and drink

There are a quarter of a million types of plants on Earth, but we cultivate only 150 of them for food. One plant family, the grasses (*Graminae*), which includes rice and cereals, feeds most of the world's population in one way or another.

The range of plant foodstuffs available has increased dramatically compared with just a few years ago. If we take just one example, bread from cereals, it is worth thinking about the huge variety on offer in shops and supermarkets. There is black pumpernickel (a sour rye bread from Germany), crusty wholemeal granary loaves containing whole wheat seeds, the long thin or squat shapes of continental breads like baguette (from France) and ciabatta (from Italy), sometimes flavoured with fruits like dates and olives.

Every part of a plant can be used for food. This is a good way to introduce the parts of plants to children (see the copiable worksheet on page 12). As far as drinks are concerned, the most obvious are tea, coffee, cocoa/chocolate, and the various drinks containing fruit extracts or flavourings. The small evergreen shrub that produces tea leaves is related to the garden camellia and has been cultivated for over 2,000 years. Over half the world's population now drinks tea. Britain consumes over 20% of the world's output each year. Without plants there would be no alcoholic drinks, based as they are on plant sugars, fermented by a fungus (yeast). There is more about plant microbes and food production in Chapter 8.

National Curriculum links:
Key Stage 1: Sc2 3b; Sc3 1a, 1c.
Key Stage 2: Sc3 1a; Sc4 2c.

Links with units in the QCA scheme of work for science:
2D Grouping and changing materials.
3C Characteristics of materials.

Before leaving the topic of food, it is worth considering new technologies that mass produce foods. Quorn® is a product, produced in vast and cheap quantities by fungi, while TVP and tofu are both extracted from soya beans – one of the fastest expanding crops currently grown in the west.

Activities

See CD-ROM:
Use of plants

- Make a collection of foods from plants for display – make sure that you include less obvious, processed types like sugars, margarine and other plant-based spreads.
- Link examples of food with the different parts of the plant that we can eat. For example, carrots and parsnips from roots, cauliflower and broccoli from flowers, saffron (from the anthers of a crocus), celery from the stem, cabbage and lettuce from leaves, sprouts from buds, onions and garlic from bulbs and ginger, potatoes from underground stems, or fruits, nuts and seeds from the plant's fruiting bodies. (See copiable worksheet 1.1 page 12.)

Figure 1.1 Edible plants

- Give children a bag of supermarket food from around the world and ask them, with the aid of a world atlas, to link the foods to different places on the map with coloured wool.
- Concentrate on one type or family of plants, e.g. the cabbage family. Make a display – link the examples of foods to parts of the plant that they come from.
- Display a variety of breads from around the world – have a tasting session.
- Show a collection of teas. Explore smells and the different coloured and sized grains. Add warm water and investigate the different colours that are obtained. Compare different teabags to find out how long infusion takes (see literacy links).

● Get children to list or collect photographs of all the different ways in which one plant, e.g. the potato, can be processed and eaten.

Protection and clothing

Cotton and linen are obvious but synthetic fibres like viscose (rayon), acetate and tri-acetate will be less obvious to children. These fabrics have all been processed from wood pulp. The stuffing of anoraks and life jackets comes from the kapok plant. The fibres are hollow and trap air, but are waterproof.

Levi Strauss first made his jeans from a plant fibre much tougher than cotton – hemp (*Cannabis sativa*). Strauss' hemp was imported from Nîmes in France – hence the word denim (*de Nîmes* in French).

Buildings

Timber has been used for buildings for at least 1,000 years. Many nomadic and semi-nomadic people still use plant materials exclusively to build temporary dwellings such as yurts. Most modern buildings still use soft woods (spruce, larch, pine) for door frames and rafters in roofs.

Household items and furnishings

Decorative woods, such as rosewood, mahogany, beech, maple, cherry and walnut, have long been valued – often used as veneers or inlays to enhance appearance of furniture. Modern manufacture favours wood dust or chip impregnated with resins (themselves derived from plants). Cork tiles, rush mats, breadboards and cutlery handles are amongst many examples of smaller household items that could be shown to children.

Transport

Rubber (latex) features in tyres and wellies, as well as condoms. It is extracted as a white milky sap bled from rainforest trees. The higher the latex percentage in rubber tyres the more stress they can take. Aircraft tyres are almost 100% latex. Latex has superb frictional qualities and this is why the soles of rock climbers' shoes are made from recycled aircraft tyres. Children could test different rubber tyre samples or types of shoes as shown on copiable worksheet 1.2. (page 13).

Figure 1.2 A Morris Minor Traveller

See CD-ROM:
Use of plants

Wood is used in boats and for decorative and structural features in cars – remember the Morris Minor Traveller? The whole frame of this car was made of wood.

Sustainable sources of fuels can be extracted from sugar cane (alcohol-based fuels), and from seed oils (biodiesel). This is one of the great hopes for future plant bio-technology.

Medicines

This is one of the most ancient uses for plants. Chinese communities around the world depend extensively on herbal remedies. A chemist in Beijing looks very different from one in this country.

Garlic is one of the most powerful natural antibiotics. Many of today's modern drugs were derived from plants. Antibiotics come from fungal extracts, e.g. penicillin from the mould that grows on some cheeses.

Natural antiseptics used to treat minor cuts and bruises include witch hazel and iodine from seaweed ash. Common illnesses and conditions often have traditional herbal remedies, e.g. camphor oil (from a Chinese evergreen tree) was popular earlier this century as a cure for colds. Flowers of evening primrose are used in treatments for PMT (pre-menstrual tension). Digitalis (from foxgloves) is still commonly used to treat heart conditions.

Drugs – use and abuse

Many of the commonly abused drugs in society today have a long history of use to relieve pain, or for ceremonial and religious purposes. Most of them have plant origins. The drug cannabis comes from hemp plants once used to make rope and clothes. Cocaine comes from the bark of the coca plant of South America; local people still chew the leaves after a hard day's work in the fields. A derivative, lignocaine, was used by dentists as an anaesthetic until quite recently. Opium and heroin come from poppies grown in the orient. LSD (acid) is refined from a rust-like fungus called ergot that grows on a species of rye grass.

Mescaline, a hallucinogenic drug from a species of cactus common in Mexico, and psilocybin (the drug in magic mushrooms) have long been used in religious ceremonies in central and south America.

Cosmetics/bathroom products

Plants in the bathroom are big business. Most soaps and hair products are made with African palm or coconut oils scented with other plant extracts and oils.

Cellulose, from wood pulp, is used as a thickener in foods as well as in cosmetics and hair products. Cellulose gum is the basis of toothpaste; peppermint of course is added for flavouring. Talcum now contains rice and maize powder as a substitute for carcinogenic mica. *Aloe vera* is very common in products, e.g. UV filtering sun screens.

The bathroom loofah is the bleached seed pod from a member of the gourd family.

Music and entertainment

We can all think of paper for books and magazines, but acetate, from wood, is the basis of all film. Think of the canvas, oils (sunflower or poppy oils probably) and pigments of paints when you next look at a painting.

Wood is used to make many musical instruments. Native bamboo is used for pan pipes. Ebony, a very hard black wood, is used for bagpipes, clarinets and billiard cues. Sycamore, maple and rosewoods are used in guitars and stringed instruments.

Sport

Willow wood is used to make cricket bats, conditioned with the extract of yet another plant, linseed. Ash is used to make hockey sticks, squash racquets and baseball bats. Hickory wood is more suited to lacrosse sticks, and persimmon (a very hard black wood) is used for the heads of golf clubs. One of the hardest types of wood known (so dense that it is one of the few types of wood that will actually sink), *Lignum vitae* was used to make crown green bowls.

The examples here are good ways of showing how one type of material, wood, is used in so many different forms depending on the strength and flexibility required. This would be a good way of teaching about the properties of materials.

In rituals, celebrations and . . . death

Woad, from a species of dock, was used as face paint in ancient British festivals. Many plant pigments for facial decorations are still used by peoples all over the world.

See CD-ROM:
Celebrations

Sandalwood and incense are burned for fragrance at religious events. Trees are often planted to commemorate people, anniversaries and events. Many species of plants and flowers are important in Asian and Jewish festivals and celebrations as we shall see in Chapter 9. And, finally, decorative woods are used for coffins. Often the quality of the wood used was seen as confirming the status of the deceased.

Figure 1.3 Plant products

See CD-ROM:
Use of plants

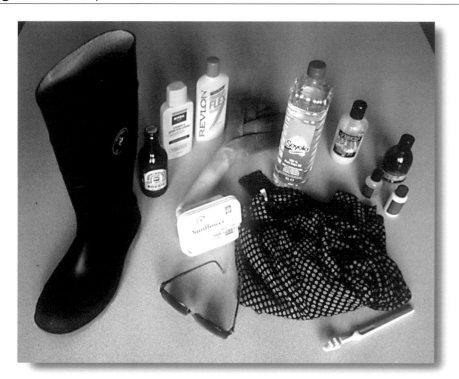

Activity

- Make a display or collage of pictures of all the products you can that come from plants.

- Ask children to draw a storyboard cartoon showing all the plant products they have had contact with since getting up and coming to school.

● Visit a supermarket. Divide the class into teams and give each team a particular area of plant products to collect examples of, e.g. clothing, sports equipment, drinks, cosmetics, leisure products, health products, etc.

Children's ideas about plant products

● Infants are unlikely to link clothes with plant origins.

● A few older juniors realise that some clothes, e.g. cotton, come from a plant. They are much more likely to mention clothing of animal origins, e.g. leather.

● Children find it difficult to trace manufactured goods back to their origins. They tend to say, for example, that " . . . things have come from another shop . . . " and that ". . . these shops got them from another bigger shop . . ."

Literacy links

Vocabulary

Key Stage 1	Key Stage 2
Bud	Alcohol
Building	Antibiotic
Drug	Cereals
Fruit	Cosmetic
Leaf	Extract
Plant	Friction
Root	Herbal
Shampoo	Latex
Soap	Margarine
Stem	Medicine
Toothpaste	Synthetic

Literacy-related activities	Most suitable for NC year
Write text/words onto a storyboard showing a child getting up and going to school that show how plants are used.	Y1/2
Encourage children to write question cards to be placed on a display or map showing food from around the world, e.g. which country do bananas come from? How many different types of food come from South America, Africa, etc?	Y2/3
Look at different types of bread and write words and phrases to describe how they look and taste.	Y3
Finish questions that could lead to investigations comparing types of tea, e.g. Are teas all the same . . . ? If we use more tea bags will the tea be . . .? Do fruity-smelling teas . . . ? Get children to write their own questions that could lead to investigations.	Y4–6

Text-related work

Fiction and poetry
Read children the story of the enormous turnip. Ask them to say which part of the plant a turnip comes from. Develop this to look at other parts of plants that we eat (KS1).

Non-fiction
Get children to list all the ways they think plants are used and to provide examples of each use. This could be tabulated. Then get children to look in a reference book such as *The Dorling Kindersley Eyewitness Guide to Plants*, (see resources section p.140) compare with their lists and extend them to include other examples (KS2).

Numeracy and information and communication technology (ICT) links

Activities related to numeracy objectives	Objectives relevant to NC year
Count and record the number of marbles needed to make a sample of rubber tyre move (non-standard measures). See activity on copiable sheet 1.2 page 13.	Y1
Record and tabulate the weight (mass) in grams or force (in Newtons) to make a sample of rubber tyre move (standard measures).	Y2–3
Sort fruits and vegetables into shape categories, e.g. round, longer than wide, pointed and round, spherical, regular and irregular.	Y2–4
Construct a pictograph to show how many children in the class prefer a particular type of tea, or to show favourite breakfast cereals in the class.	Y3

ICT links	Relating to QCA unit
Make word labels for parts of a plant using a word processor and hang them onto a real plant or a display.	1D
Find clip art showing various fruits, vegetables and food items. Cut and paste them onto a picture of a plant to show what part they have come from.	3A, 4D

Eat it all up

What part of a plant does each of these foods come from?
Write your answers in the box next to each drawing.

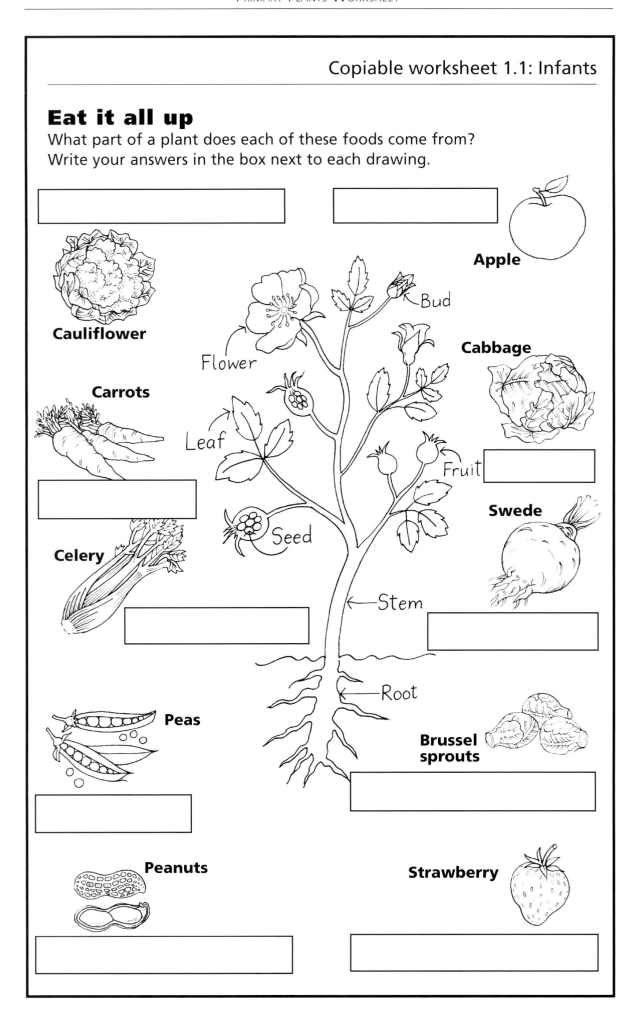

Apple

Cauliflower

Flower

Bud

Cabbage

Carrots

Leaf

Fruit

Swede

Seed

Celery

Stem

Root

Peas

Brussel sprouts

Peanuts

Strawberry

Tyre force

Which type of tyre has the most grip?

- Look at the types of tyre you are given.
- Which ones will have most grip? Give reasons for your choices.
- Test each type by adding marbles to the pot until the tyre moves.

Make sure you keep your test fair. How will you do this?

- Now put your results into this table:

Type of tyre	Number of marbles added to the pot

- Draw a bar chart of your results:

Number of marbles in pot

Types of tyre

- Which type of tyre had most grip? How can you tell?
- How did your results compare with your prediction?

14

Chapter 2

Variety is the spice of plant life

THERE ARE over a quarter of a million plant species on Earth and tropical rainforests hold about half of them. Who knows what future sources of food and medicines essential for our survival lie deep in the rainforests – what's left of them? Knowing about and conserving this variety may be essential to our survival.

Plant variety is greatest where conditions are benign; but our little temperate island off the coast of northern Europe contains a remarkable range of plants, thanks mainly to various imports over the ages. The Romans brought onions, figs and vines to remind them of home when they got a posting to the 'frozen north'. Explorers visiting foreign lands brought back exotic plants like the potato from North America (Sir Walter Raleigh), apricots and lilac from Spain, rhododendrons and azaleas from the shores of the Black Sea, hydrangeas from China, and acacia trees from Australia.

Many of our common park and garden plants arrived in a great flurry of activity during the 19th century. Flowering currant and Californian poppy were imported from North America; flowering cherry from Japan; jasmine, forsythia and chrysanthemum from the Far East; and primula, lilies and gentians from Asia.

Not all imports have been beneficial to our environment and we will be looking at some examples of this in Chapter 7.

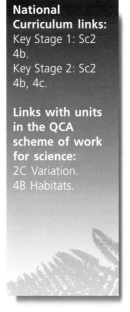

National Curriculum links:
Key Stage 1: Sc2 4b.
Key Stage 2: Sc2 4b, 4c.

Links with units in the QCA scheme of work for science:
2C Variation.
4B Habitats.

See CD-ROM:
Flowers

Variety or variation?

Textbooks and schemes of work often mention these terms together. Children (and their teachers) often mix them up, so it is important to understand the difference.

Variety is concerned with the diversity of different species of living things. In other words, how many different types there are. In primary science we use activities to help children understand this, such as: grouping living things; looking at similarities and differences; and using keys to sort and identify types.

Variation is concerned with the subtle differences between individuals within one species. These differences result from the unique genetic make-up inherited by each living thing. It would be wrong to talk about the variation of different types of trees in a wood – this is variety (or more properly diversity); but it is all right to talk about the variations in leaf sizes and heights of just the oak trees in the wood.

Variety within the plant world

Plants were the first colonists of land over 300 million years ago and they now occupy even the most inhospitable habitats, from the frozen wastes of Antarctica to the hot springs of New Zealand and Wyoming. Plants have diversified and evolved into a huge range of forms, both with and without flowers. Unfortunately, children rarely see plants as anything other than brightly coloured (flowering), potted varieties (as the children's ideas section on page 18 shows). This means that we have a lot of work to do in showing them that there are some wonderful plants out there to get excited about.

You may be surprised to know that of the 275,000 types of plants on the planet, many do not have flowers. These groups do not reproduce themselves from seeds but from spores. There are five main groups:

- algae
- mosses
- liverworts
- ferns
- lichens

See CD-ROM:
Flowerless plants

Algae include all the microscopic plants that live in water and land and are the starting point for food chains in oceans, lakes, rivers and ponds. Not all algae are small. The largest water plant of all is an alga, the giant kelp seaweed of California. It grows up to 65 metres in length, and so fast that they say you can actually watch it grow.

Mosses and liverworts are two further groups of non-flowering plants. Both are small low-growing, shrubby types. Mosses have rows of almost transparent, thin leaflets, and can hold water like a sponge, while liverworts have a fleshy body without obvious leaves. Both are found in shady, damp places where their sex cells can be fertilised after it rains. Ferns are some of the more obvious non-flowering plants and are common houseplants. The spore-producing organs beneath the fronds (note – not leaves) can often be seen as brown, raised ridges or circles. Bracken is a common woodland example. Ferns were the most common land plants 250 million years ago, and they grew in huge river delta swamps. As the conditions changed, the swamps were engulfed by sediments and, millions of years later, we extract their remains as coal.

The final group is the lichens. These are unusual plants; really associations between fungi, extracting nutrients from the surroundings, and algae, which photosynthesise to make food. They are one of the most important plants of the fragile arctic tundra, and food for reindeer.

See CD-ROM: *Fungi*

In the past, botanists sometimes included a sixth group, fungi, as plants and it is important not to forget them here. The more familiar examples are mushrooms and toadstools, but the group also includes all the types of moulds that grow on food and the commercially important yeasts that are used in bread-making and production of alcoholic beverages. We will return to this group in Chapter 8.

Figure 2.1 Examples of non-flowering plants

Lichens and mosses growing on trees

See CD-ROM: *Flowerless plants*

Fern leaf: close up

Kelp seaweed – an alga

True flowering plants include the familiar wild and garden plants, with their bright flowers. But it is important to realise that many flowering types have insignificant, dull flowers, including many trees and all grasses.

One group of flowering plants is special because the seeds are not held in fruiting bodies, but in special cones. These are the coniferous trees, or cone-bearers, and are amongst the most ancient of flowering land plants.

Activities: Variety of plants – Key Stage 1

(See also copiable worksheet 2.1)

- Encourage young children to name as many types of plants as they can.
- Take them on a visit to a garden centre or supermarket. Go around the school and the school grounds. What colours and shapes of plants can they see?
- Provide some examples of real plants for children. Include non-flowering types like mosses and ferns. Also include pictures or examples of trees, cacti, grasses and pond plants, which are less obvious as plants to children. Ask them to comment on similarities and differences. Use sorting hoops to sort the plants into different types.
- Make a collection of fruits and/or vegetables and ask children to group them in various ways.
- Children could be helped to cut various fruits and vegetables (both lengthways and crossways) and make paint prints for display.

Children's ideas about plant variety

- Young children may not even think that plants are alive.
- Children are less aware of the names of plant groups than of animal groups.
- When asked to name plants, children often choose types with obvious bright, large flowers and houseplants.
- Children often group plants according to where they are found and what they generally look like, e.g. ". . . moss and this grass go together because they are found close to the ground . . ."

Plant variation

In the last century an Austrian monk called Gregor Mendel*, a keen gardener, experimented with pea plant varieties. He found that tall plants that were bred with short ones gave a mixture of tall and short types, but always in the same ratio (three tall ones to every short one). From his results he guessed that a pair of factors determined shortness or tallness in pea plants, with tallness dominating shortness. He found that this also held true for the colour and texture of the pea's seeds. What he didn't know then, but we do now, is that these factors are actually pairs of genes held on one part of one chromosome in the pollen and ovules of the pea plants. The combination of the genes in a new individual is down to which ones are inherited following fertilisation of an ovule by a pollen grain (this process is explained fully in chapter 6, page 67).

Many of the variations that Mendel studied are termed *discontinuous*. This means either one thing or another – flowers are white or blue; seeds have wrinkled or smooth coats – there are no in-betweens. The environment has little effect on the outcome. This type of variation is actually less common than *continuous* variation where there can be a range of types between two extremes, e.g. a range of sizes of leaves. These variations are controlled by several pairs of genes located on different parts of a chromosome. The full expression of the inherited characteristics is much more likely to be influenced by the environment. If a plant has inherited a number of genes which would normally make it tall, it might not end up *being* tall if it doesn't get enough nutrients from the soil, or is growing in an exposed, windy site.

The number of recombinations of genes that can take place following fertilisation, and hence the number of variations in plants, is staggering. It has been estimated that every time an apple tree is fertilised, the number of potential variations is 131,000. It was just as well that Mendel investigated with the simpler discontinuous variations in his peas, or the science of genetics might never have got going.

Variation means that plant breeders and food companies can select features that are of benefit to them. If you want nice small peas to put in a can, you want peas of a uniform size and pods that ripen at the same time, so that harvesting is easier and cheaper. The plant breeder will therefore select over a number of generations the pea plants with these features, and breed only from them.

This selective breeding of plants has been going on for a very long time. Five-thousand-year-old pottery found in the Middle East shows barley with only two rows of seed per seed-head. Today's varieties have at least six rows of seed. Modifying a plant's genetics to produce more food is not a new science.

* For more information on the life and works of George Mendel, see *Famous Scientists and Inventors* by John Davis (Questions Publishing, 2000).

Activities: Plant variation – Key Stage 2

- Give children a number of vegetables of one type, e.g. potatoes, onions, carrots, pea pods. Share them out among the class.

Note: try to select garden or organically-grown types because the variation will be wider as they have not been graded for size and bagged for sale in shops.

If you use fast plants (see next chapter) you can measure the lengths of pods on plants of the same age.

- Get the children to measure one variable showing continuous variation: length or weight for example.

You could also do the same with other examples of variation such as leaf size and height of plants, but these are more likely to be influenced by environmental factors (see Chapter 7).

- Collect results from the class into size classes and get children to draw a histogram of the results. Children could use a computer for this (see ICT links).

A *histogram* is a special kind of bar graph where the bars are allowed to touch because the measurements have all been taken from a population where variation runs continuously between two extremes. In all other types of bar chart, the bars must not touch because the measurements are taken from variations that are discrete or categoric – there can be no in-betweens.

Figure 2.2 A histogram showing variation in the weights of potatoes

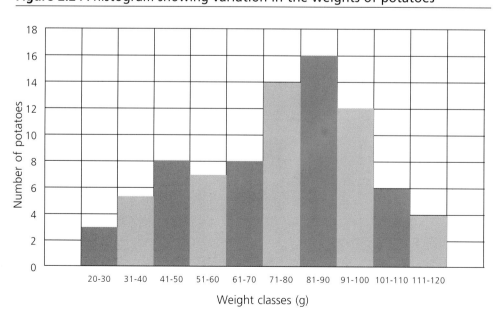

Figure 2.2 shows an example of a histogram that could be plotted.

Other variations that could be investigated:

- The number of petals on daisy flowers;
- The number of seeds in a pod (fast plants are good for this – see page 27).

In both these cases the graph needed is a *bar graph* with categories separated – you cannot have 6.5 peas in a pod.

Figure 2.3 A bar chart showing variation in the numbers of petals on flowers of daisy plants

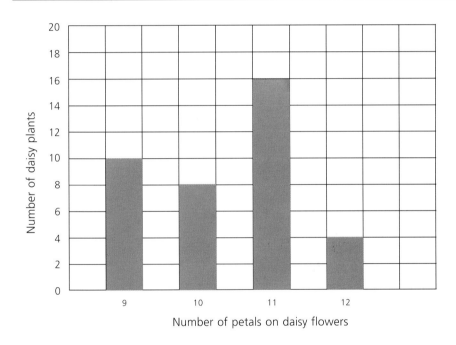

Number of petals on daisy flowers

(y-axis: Number of daisy plants)

- You could also investigate the relationship between one variation and another (see copiable worksheet 2.2).

For example:

- Do the longest pods have the greatest number of seeds in them?
- Do the tallest plants have the largest leaves?

In this case the graph needed is a *scattergraph*, because you are plotting one set of continuously variable data against another. Many computer graph drawing packages have the facility to draw this type of graph for you (see ICT links).

Figure 2.4 A scattergraph showing the relationship between the number of seeds and length of seed pod

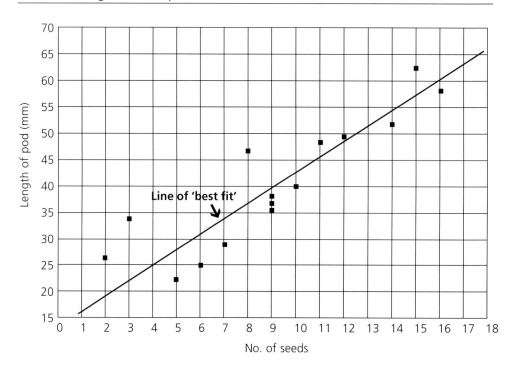

Children's ideas about plant variation

- Young children do not realise the causes of variation. They see living things as different because they are "just born that way".
- Older children often think that variation results from environmental change – plants change to suit the environment.
- Sometimes children think that variations change with age as plants grow.

Literacy links

Vocabulary	
Key Stage 1	*Key Stage 2*
Cone	Algae
Fern	Conifer
Flower	Deciduous
Moss	Evergreen
Vegetable	Gene
	Lichens
	Liverwort
	Rhododendron
	Spore
	Sycamore
	Variation
	Variety

Literacy-related activities	Most suitable for NC year
Get children to list the colours and shapes of flowers, vegetables or fruit as they visit a supermarket or garden centre.	R/Y1
Encourage children to use an increasingly wide range of descriptive words and phrases to compare plant leaves and the ways they vary, e.g. descriptions of shape, colour and tone, hairiness, serrated or smooth edges, patterns and colours of veins, etc.	Y2–4
Ask children to look up definitions for terms such as deciduous, evergreen, coniferous and spore, in dictionaries and glossaries. Get children to consult books, encyclopaedias or databases to find examples of trees that are coniferous. Ask children if more than one term can apply to a tree, e.g. can a tree be described as *both* evergreen and coniferous?	Y2–6 (Depending on terms used)

Text-related work

Fiction and poetry
Read the poem *Trees* by Sara Coleridge to children (see Chapter 11 page 145). Get children to write their own poems, starting each line with the name of a different type of plant (KS2).

Non-fiction
Consult texts and databases to find the names of plants introduced to Britain, when they were imported and who introduced them (KS2).

Numeracy and information and communication technology (ICT) links

Activities related to numeracy objectives	Objectives relevant to NC year
Collect potatoes or pea pods (organically grown are best) and put them in size order from smallest to largest. Ask children how many are smaller or larger than a particular specimen.	R/Y1
Work out areas of leaf shapes from different bushes using squared paper. The findings could be displayed as *bar graphs* showing leaf variation for plants of the same type growing in different areas, e.g. on north-, south- and west-facing parts of the school.	Y4
Children in groups could measure the length of leaves, pods or fruits from one plant. Collect measurements from each group of children. Get children to group the measurements into size classes, e.g. 4–6cm, 7–9cm, 10–12cm, etc.	Y6
Get children to produce a frequency graph (histogram) showing the results of an investigation like the one above, and ask them to find the *mode* (most common length), the *median* (middle value), and *mean* (average) for length.	Y6

ICT links	Relating to QCA unit
Enter results of measurements like those above into a spreadsheet and get children to produce the correct graph to display data. For example, a *bar graph* for categoric data – leaf area of plants growing on different sides of the school. A *frequency chart* or *histogram* to show size classes of leaves on one type of plant. A *scattergraph* for trends in one factor plotted against another, e.g. do the largest pods contain the most seeds?	4D, 5D
Ask pupils to search databases and encyclopaedias on the Internet or on CD-ROM to find information about plants introduced to Britain.	2C, 4D

Are they plants?

Which of these are plants? Circle the ✓ or ✗.

If you know any of the names of the plants, write them above the drawings

Plant? ✓ or ✗   Plant? ✓ or ✗   Plant? ✓ or ✗

Plant? ✓ or ✗   Plant? ✓ or ✗   Plant? ✓ or ✗

Plant? ✓ or ✗   Plant? ✓ or ✗   Plant? ✓ or ✗

Do the tallest plants have the largest leaves?

You will need to measure the size (length or width) of at least *three* leaves on six *different* plants.

You could use plants growing around the school, in a field or meadow, or ones given to you by your teacher BUT they must all be of the **same type**.

- Why must they all be of the **same type**?
- Record the height of your plant and the size of three of its leaves.
- Which leaves will you measure? Where will they come from on the plant? Does it matter which ones you choose each time?
- How will you work out an average? Why is it important to do this?
- Record your results in a table like this:

Height of the plant in cm	Lengths or widths of three leaves			Average size of leaves
	Leaf 1	Leaf 2	Leaf 3	

You could put your results together with results from other groups – as long as you have measured the same type of plant.

- Now draw a graph of *the height of plants against the average length or width of leaves.*
- What type of graph will you draw?
- What will you plot along the horizontal axis and along the vertical axis?
- Plot your graph onto squared paper and mark each plot clearly with a cross. You could use a computer to draw the graph for you.
- Can you see a trend or pattern in your results?
- Draw a line to fit through the crosses on your graph to show the pattern – if you think you have one.
- Explain any pattern in your results. Is this what you expected?

Chapter 3

Carry on growing

O**F ALL** the areas of plant activity studied in schools this is most teachers' favourite. There is a rich range of ideas and activities to draw on and you can be creative here. You can do far more than just germinating a few cress seeds in pots! Work on growth in schools often begins and ends with germination, but it is important to extend children's experience beyond this. The new technology of *fast plants* now provides a feasible way to show children the complete life cycle of plants within a short topic.

National Curriculum links: Key Stage 1: Sc2 1c, 3a, 3b, 3c.
Key Stage 2: Sc2 1b, 3a, 3c.

Links with units in the QCA scheme of work for science:
1B Growing plants.
2B Plants and animals in the local environment.
3B Helping plants grow well.

The seed: an amazing little package of life

Plants invest their futures in seeds. Each seed contains an embryo with its inherited set of genes, and a food store to start the plant off until it can support itself by making its own food. Seeds have to be tough to withstand harsh conditions, and attacks by animals. Their survival can be astonishing. A seed dug up from the arctic tundra germinated after being frozen for 10,000 years. Seeds of desert plants regularly last for decades waiting for the rain that signals time for germination.

The preservation of seeds is a way in which the diversity of the world's plants can be stored. At the Royal Botanic Gardens at Kew, a millennium seed bank is being created to preserve the world's most endangered plants. The seeds are carefully dried and then deep frozen. Most will remain viable for 200 years, to be grown again if the species is in trouble. Keep your own seeds in school cool and dry with a sachet of silica gel inside an airtight tin, and they should be useable the following year.

Starting off

Germination relies on a complex set of triggers. If the seed germinates before the conditions are right, the plant's investment is wasted. There are three environmental conditions that are important to set off the changes involved in germination.

See CD-ROM:
Plant activities

Temperature: controls the moment at which chemical reactions inside the seed start and the rate at which they will continue. The temperature at which germination starts reflects where the plant comes from. Growing citrus fruits like lemons and oranges, accustomed to warm southern European climates, means that you have to soak seeds in warm water to stimulate germination.

Water: the food stored in the seed must be moved to and around new tissues in a liquid.

Air: like all life, the growing seedling must 'burn' sugars from the seed's food store using oxygen from the air. The energy released is used to power growth of the seedling plant until it has enough green leaves to make its own food by photosynthesis (see chapter 4 page 39 for a fuller explanation).

See CD-ROM: *Plant activities*

Children (and adults) often fail to realise that air is important, and give seeds little chance to get going when they over-water them. A water-logged soil is one where the soil's natural air spaces are filled with water. The seed literally suffocates. Another common misconception (see section showing children's ideas) is that seeds need light to germinate. If you think about it, most seeds have to germinate in relative darkness covered by soil. If you germinate seeds in total darkness, seedling plants actually grow faster than ones kept in the light. This is because of a sudden rush of growth hormone in the stem. The resulting seedlings have thin, straggly stems with yellow leaves and are said to be *etiolated.*

Figure 3.1 A geranium plant that has been growing in the dark

You might be wondering why seeds and bulbs don't get off to a false start if the soil suddenly warms up in autumn or early spring. Most plants in northern climes have evolved mechanisms so that the plant will not respond until exposed to a long period of cold. The seed can

time whether it has been through a winter. Bulb sellers fool hyacinths into flowering at Christmas by keeping them in cold conditions over the summer months.

For the seed to germinate, water must be able to enter a small hole called the *micropyle* in the tough protective seed coat. In nature, seed coats get worn down by abrasion against the soil particles making it easier for water to enter in the spring. Seeds out of a packet may need a little help. Gardeners often nick the coat of seeds like the sweet pea with a knife to get them going. One of nature's toughest seeds was from a 1,000 year old lotus tree – scientists had to remove the seed coat with sulphuric acid to get it to germinate.

Two types of germination

In the early stages of germination the seed root (*radicle*) emerges from the embryo inside the seed and sends out delicate side roots and root hairs in search of moisture. Then the *plumule*, the seedling's shoot, emerges and, depending on the type of plant, either struggles free leaving the remains of the seed attached underground (*hypogeal germination*), or drags the seed with it as it pushes upwards into the air (*epigeal germination*).

Figure 3.2 The two types of germination

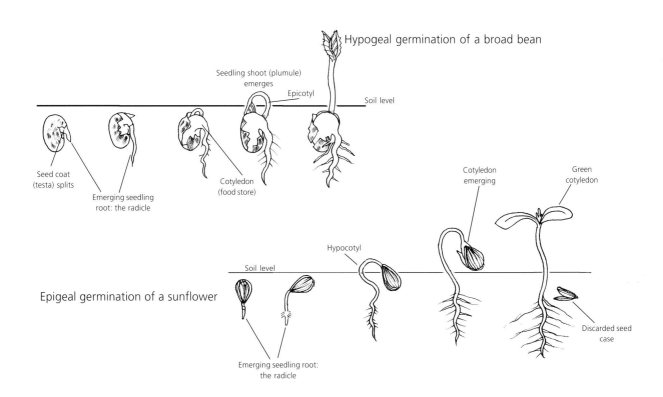

Activities: Exploring germination

See CD-ROM:
Plant activities

- Ask children to draw what they think is inside a seed.
- A good way for children to study germination is for them to see what's going on by germinating different types of seeds inside plastic bottles (see copiable sheet 3.1 on page 37).

Make sure that you include seeds showing both types of germination – broad beans and peas work well for hypogeal germination, but make sure that you soak them first for about 24 hours. Sunflower seeds are good examples for epigeal germination (you could always plant them out in the school garden or in pots later).

- Stick centimetre tape on the side of the germination bottle or let children mark their own measuring scale. Growth can be recorded in a table along with a diary of drawings showing significant changes.

Progressive growth over a period of time should be graphed as a *line graph*. This is because you are graphing change in one continuous variable against change in another. This makes the fourth type of graph children should be familiar with in primary science (KS2) – we met the other types in Chapter 2.

Figure 3.3 A line graph showing the growth of a plant

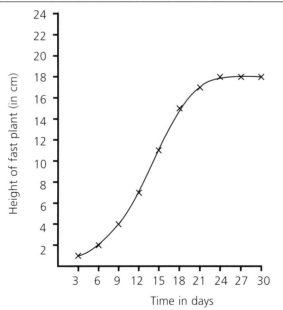

- Try putting broad bean seeds upside down and sideways to see how they germinate (KS2).
- Get children to list variables that they think might affect germination. They could try altering:
  — the amount of water added;
  — where they keep them – temperature and light;

> — the depth of compost put above the seeds;
> — the type of planting medium – try sand, vermiculite (an inert growing medium available from most garden centres), paper towels, cotton wool, potting compost.

Use fast germinating seeds for this, e.g. mustard and cress, mung beans or chick peas. Any small containers will be adequate – old egg boxes make a good alternative to pots, but make sure that children keep the top of the growth medium just damp so that seeds do not dry out.

- Children can try germinating interesting seeds from fruits such as lemons and oranges, but these will need soaking in tepid water for a few days first (look back at the section 'Starting off' on page 27 to find out why).

Children's ideas about germination and growth

- Many children think that seeds need soil to germinate.

This isn't always true. Some crop plants, like tomatoes, are grown using hydroponics – just in a broth of nutrients and water. Plants do, however, need the soil as their rootlets grow for support and as a source of nutrient minerals.

- Many children think that light is required for germination.
- Some children believe that an entire plant exists within the seed and that germination and subsequent growth involves an unfolding process.
- Few children are aware that growth is continuous. Many of them think that plants only grow at certain times, e.g. at night, in summer or when conditions are right.
- Very few children realise that growth beyond germination involves the addition of new material (as new mass) produced by the plant.

You can prove this by drying and then weighing plants of different ages. The reason for drying the plant is that children might think that all of the added mass has come from water rather than from new tissues (KS2).

Growing up – looking at the further growth of plants

The story of growth does not begin and end with germination, and it is important for children to track the changes that take place so they can appreciate the full picture. This will help tackle some of the misconceptions that children have (the section above). *Fast plants* provide an effective way of doing this.

Using fast plants

These are a type of turnip plant selectively bred to complete its life cycle from seed to seed in 30 days or less. They were originally grown in the USA for research purposes, but local schools soon cottoned on and they were developed as a teaching resource. Fast plant technology has been around in secondary schools in the UK for about ten years and is now making its appearance in primary schools. Because the life cycle is so fast, they are excellent for helping children to study growth, take measurements and record significant events like flowering, pollination and appearance of the first seed pods.

You need a bank of fluorescent light tubes as the plants have to grow under permanent light. The seeds are sown in little polystyrene pots containing a 1:1 mix of vermiculite and potting compost. The pots have a wick of capillary matting sticking out of their bases and stand on a capillary watering system contained in old margarine tubs for easy maintenance. Full instructions on building light banks and planting, growing and maintaining fast plants can be obtained from the organisations and suppliers mentioned in Chapter 11 page 148.

When flowers start appearing (about 15 days), they will need pollinating and, in the absence of bees, children have to do this. It helps if they make a buzzing noise as they transfer pollen from one flower to another because botanists have found that sound vibrations help pollen detach from anthers.

Fast plant technology is supported by the organisation SAPS. They run training courses on using the resource and if you sign up you get an excellent newsletter containing ideas for plant experiments that you can carry out with your class (details are provided in Chapter 11 page 148).

See CD-ROM:
Plant activities

Figure 3.4 Fast plants of different ages

Grassheads – being creative with growth
(see copiable sheet 3.2)

Figure 3.5 Some examples of grassheads

These are easy to make, fun and have some sound scientific points that can be taught using them.

Make sure that you use fresh grass seed as its viability from year to year is quite low. It is important to keep the top of your grasshead quite moist until the grass begins to germinate – usually within ten days. Grassheads can also be made using empty egg shells.

Activities: using grassheads

- Try making a cresshead – if you use tights you will have to poke holes in the mesh to let the germinating seedlings through.
- What will happen if you give your grasshead a haircut? Will the grass grow back again?
- What about a cresshead? Will the cress grow back again (KS2)?

The science behind this is quite neat. Grass has a growing point at its base and so cutting it does not cut off the supply of chemicals that control growth – this is why cutting your lawn doesn't stop the grass growing. Cress has a growing point near the tip of the stem – if you cut it off it cannot grow another one.

Literacy links

Vocabulary

Key Stage 1	Key Stage 2
Bean	Compost
Bulb	Embryo
Cold	Life cycle
Grow	Root – hair
Heat	Survival
Seed	Temperature
Shoot	
Soil	
Sunflower	

Literacy-related activities	Most suitable for NC year
Ask children to sequence stages of germination and growth using drawings or photographs.	Y1
Give children six words about germination and growth and ask them to arrange them alphabetically. Fold an A4 (landscape) sheet of paper three times and enter each word and its letter with a simple explanation of the word into each section.	Y2
Use a concept map where words on cards such as *seed, root, shoot, soil, water, warmth, sun, grow* can be joined by other words to make sentences, e.g. A *seed* needs *warmth* to *grow*.	Y2
Encourage children to write about their investigations into conditions for seed growth using a variety of openers, e.g. We were trying to find out if . . . The best conditions to germinate a seed were . . . We could tell because . . .	Y3/4
Get children to write a sequence of instructions and see if another group can follow them, e.g. how to make a grasshead. Children could design a plant care label using symbols and instructions describing the plant's needs.	Y4/5
Get children to write *labels* for each part of the story of germination and growth of a plant and to add pockets or slide-out cards that reveal *captions* explaining what is happening at each stage. This could be part of a wall display.	Y5
Children could present information on how to grow seeds or plants as a poster or advert. Ask children to write a warning poster on the subject of 'Killing your plants with kindness' (by over-watering).	Y5/6

Text-related work

Fiction and poetry
The Tiny Seed by Eric Carle (see Chapter 11 page 140) provides an excellent context for children to talk about their science explorations into conditions for germinating seeds (KS1).

Encourage children to write poems. Highlight each line of the poem using captions or labels, e.g. about the life story of a plant (KS1/2).

Non-fiction
Children could use gardening books and seed packets to look up the ways different seeds should be planted. They could make a planting calendar for flowers and vegetables based on information from books (KS2).

Numeracy and information and communications technology (ICT) links

Activities related to numeracy objectives	Objectives relevant to NC year
Open up seed pods and count the seeds up to 10 or 20.	R/Y1
Say whether there are enough or too many seeds to plant in a pot.	Y2
Sort fruits or seeds into different shapes and develop mathematical vocabulary, e.g. round, long, thin, curved.	Y2
Devise and use a tally system: i.e. ⦀⦀ = 5, and record seeds in pods and fruits containing large numbers of seeds, e.g. sweet peppers. Encourage children to use conventions such as < and > to compare numbers of seeds in different fruits.	Y4
Record the heights of growing plants and work out growth rate in centimetres or millimetres per day.	Y5
Identify the period of most rapid growth of a seedling from a line graph.	Y6

ICT links	Relating to QCA unit
Type labels for each part of the germination process from a word bank (and use in activities suggested in the literacy links).	1B, 1D
Record the number of seeds germinating out of 10-20 in different conditions, using a pictograph.	1E
Take photographs with a digital camera or use those on the CD-ROM showing different stages of growth, and paste these into a word-processed account or story about germination.	3A
Devise questions about seeds and germination, e.g. Which is the world's largest seed? Which seed can live the longest? Post questions via email to a science expert.	3E, 5B
Enter results of growth measurements for each day onto a spreadsheet and select the right type of graph to show changes in patterns of growth, e.g. a line graph – see the activities section.	4D

Copiable worksheet 3.1: Infants and lower juniors

Making a germination bottle

1. Cut off the top part of a pop bottle. Ask an adult to help you with this.

2. Cut out a piece of card to fit inside the bottle and cover it with kitchen towel.

3. Push the card into the bottle and make it a tight fit.

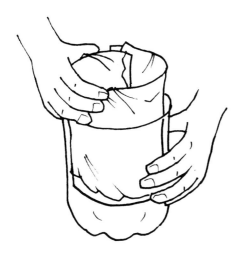

4. Now drop a seed between the plastic of the bottle and the card so that it is trapped about half way down. You can add different seeds around the rest of the bottle.

5. Now add water – but be careful that it comes well below the seeds.

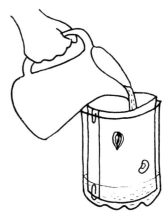

6. Now watch your seeds grow. You could keep a diary to show what happens. You could measure your seedlings to see how much they have grown.

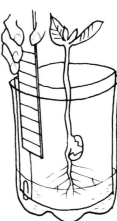

Copiable worksheet 3.2: Infants and lower juniors

Making a grasshead

1. Cut off the 'foot' from an old pair of tights.

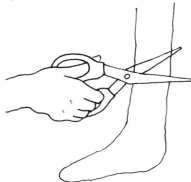

2. Put a teaspoon of grass-seed into the foot and add a tablespoon of compost.

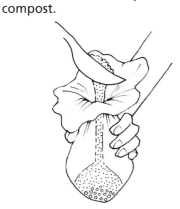

3. Now fill the tights with something that will soak up water. Make sure that you stuff the foot until it makes a ball shape.

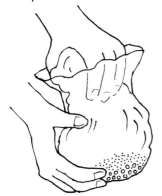

4. Now tie up the open end of the tights to make a 'grasshead'. Soak your grasshead in water.

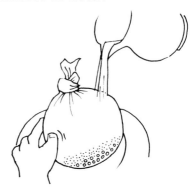

5. Put your grasshead onto a pot of water with the grass seed at the top. Fill the pot with water.

6. You can add decoration like a nose and eyes.

Now sit back and watch the grass grow.

Give your grasshead a 'haircut' when you think it needs it! Will its 'hair' grow back again?

Chapter 4

Feeding the world

WITHOUT PLANTS there would be no life or food on Earth. Even the Inuit peoples of the Arctic, total meat eaters, depend ultimately on plants for their food. The seals and fish they hunt have eaten animals who in turn ate smaller invertebrates that fed on the green algae floating in the sea.

Plants and a few bacteria are the only living things capable of making their own food from simple substances around them. The scale of the operation is amazing. An acre of corn can produce the equivalent of 10,000 bags of sugar in one year. It has been estimated that the total energy in the sugars produced by the world's plants in just 10 days is the same as the energy stored in our current reserves of coal, gas and oil.

The process of food making in plants is called *photosynthesis* and plants need just air (carbon dioxide), water and sunlight energy to do it. This basic process, however, seems difficult for most people to accept. Graduates from one of the USA's leading science universities, the Massachusetts Institute of Technology, were given a wooden log and asked if they thought it came mainly from the air. The same question was asked of future primary teachers graduating from a top university in the UK. Hardly anyone thought the log could have come mainly from the air – most thought that substances from the soil formed the bulk of the wood (see the section indicating children's ideas, below). This is typical of the problems we face as teachers. We not only have to take on board the natural misconceptions that children bring to lessons, but also to resolve our own mental models of how the world works. These are based on intuitive ideas and observations from life. After all we buy plant food in the garden centre, so it is no surprise that we assume this is the main food that plants need.

National Curriculum links:
Key Stage 2: Sc2 1b, 1c, 3a, 3b, 5b, 5d, 5e.

Links with units in the QCA scheme of work for science:
3B Helping plants grow well.
4B Habitats.
6A Interdependence and adaptation.

Children's ideas about how plants get their food

- Children often think that plants get their food from the soil or from plant food that we give them.
- Older children (and adults) often think that plants make food in the day and breathe in oxygen only at night.

Breathing – we really mean *respiration* – is a continuous process and does not stop. Plants, like all living things, take in oxygen to respire (burn-up) sugars to provide them with energy. This process releases carbon dioxide. The confusion comes when we think about photosynthesis, which requires carbon dioxide, and releases oxygen as a waste product during the day. In many ways photosynthesis is the exact opposite of respiration.

Leaves as food factories

Carbon dioxide from the air and the hydrogen part of a water molecule are the raw materials for everything a plant makes including all its woody tissues, leaves, flowers – the lot. The next time you look at your dining table or a wooden chair – that's all there was to start with.

The energy for this incredible process comes from sunlight. The light is trapped by a special molecule, *chlorophyll*, held in disc-like structures in leaf cells called *chloroplasts*. The sunlight's energy is used to split the hydrogen atoms from water molecules and the hydrogen is used to reduce the carbon dioxide to produce sugar. The oxygen from the water is wasted and breathed out into the air through pores mainly on the lower surface of the leaves. So the waste of plant food-making refreshes the stores of oxygen that life has extracted for respiration – this is why we sometimes refer to the great forests as 'the lungs of the Earth'.

Figure 4.1 This diagram summarises what goes on in leaves

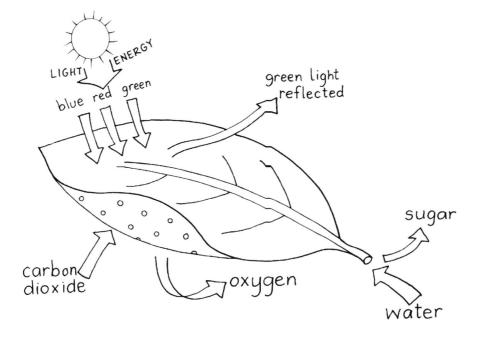

Activity: Measuring photosynthesis (KS2)

In the primary school it is not desirable or necessary to teach the full process of photosynthesis, but children do need to know that plants can make their own food. The traditional way to demonstrate that leaves have made food is to test them to see if starch is present. This requires chemicals and techniques that are NOT suitable in the primary classroom.

Another way of observing food making by leaves is to measure the amount of oxygen produced. You can do this by cutting out leaf discs and putting them into a syringe filled with a solution of sodium hydrogen carbonate (baking soda). The air in the spaces between cells in the leaves is sucked out and the discs sink. When they make food again, oxygen fills the leaf spaces and the discs become less dense and more buoyant, so they float to the top. (See copiable sheet 4.1)

The time it takes for them to float is therefore a measure of the rate at which they are making food.

If you haven't got fast plants or a light bank, the leaves of mustard rape (found in many supermarkets) and the strong light from an overhead projector will do.

How efficient are plants?

Plants are at the start of most food chains. They are the providers, or in ecological terms, the *producers*. Leaves are the plant's food factories, but how efficient are they at manufacturing food and how much energy in food they make is passed along a food chain? In other words – how much energy falling on grass ends up in a beefburger? The answer is not very much, as you can see from Figure 4.2.

Does this mean that we would all be better off, energy wise, being vegetarian? It is true that producing a tonne of beef requires far more energy than a tonne of wheat. Add to this the energy bills for fertiliser used on pasture and for maintaining and housing cattle, and more energy bills for packing and processing the meat, and there is certainly food for thought.

Clever leaves

As only small amounts of light energy from the sun are available for food making, plants have had to invest a great deal of their evolution in clever designs for light collection. Plants make sure that each leaf

See CD-ROM:
Leaf forms

Figure 4.2 How much of the sun's energy ends up in a beefburger?

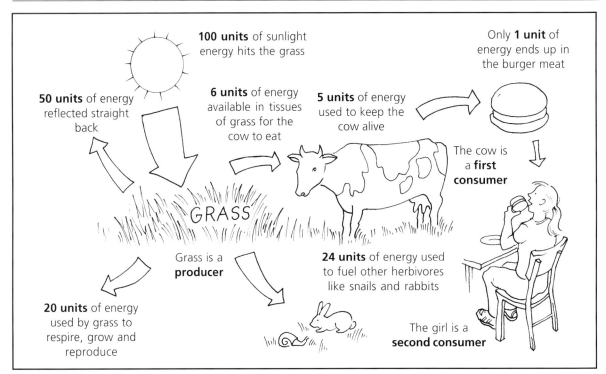

100 units of sunlight energy hits the grass

Only **1 unit** of energy ends up in the burger meat

50 units of energy reflected straight back

6 units of energy available in tissues of grass for the cow to eat

5 units of energy used to keep the cow alive

The cow is a **first consumer**

GRASS

Grass is a **producer**

24 units of energy used to fuel other herbivores like snails and rabbits

The girl is a **second consumer**

20 units of energy used by grass to respire, grow and reproduce

gets as much light as possible through every daylight hour. If you look at the arrangements of leaves on a plant, you will see that there is hardly any overlap – no leaf is shaded by its neighbour.

See CD-ROM: *Leaf forms*

Under the leaf canopy of forests and woods the light can be so dim that plants have to use additional strategies. Some leaves are very large to collect the maximum amount of light. The arum lily of South East Asia holds the record – its leaf can be three metres across – the whole thing covering about five square metres. The huge fan-shaped leaves of cycads are another way of collecting the broken light filtering through

Figure 4.3 Examples of arrangements of leaves

Spiral arrangement   Fan shape (umbrella grass)   Opposite and alternate (parlour palm)

the canopy. Climbers like cheese plants in the rainforests have given up the chase for light on the forest floor and spiral upwards to grab what light they can on their large, broad leaves.

Figure 4.4 Large leaves of rainforest plants

See CD-ROM:
Leaf forms

Plants cannot use all the sunlight energy hitting their leaves. Light is made up of many different wavelengths or colours – the colours of the rainbow. Blue and red light have more energy than green, and this is what the plants absorb. Begonias (common as houseplants in the UK) living on the floor of tropical forests get every type of light available. The underside of their leaves is red, so the high energy wavelengths of light (blues) that get through the leaf are reflected back to the chlorophyll in the top of the leaf. Some species of begonias have tiny lenses on the upper skin of their leaves to help focus light rays onto the chlorophyll-packed cells below.

See CD-ROM:
Tropical

In deep water plants have even less light available, but since blue light has a shorter wavelength than red, it can penetrate to greater depths. Seaweeds living in deep water are often red so that they can absorb what little blue light reaches them.

See CD-ROM:
Flowerless plants

Activities: Looking at leaf design (KS2)

- Carry out a survey of plant leaf shapes and arrangements inside and around the school. Record all the different leaf shapes and the ways they are arranged on plants (you could use a digital camera for this).
- Put the shapes or arrangements into categories. How many plants have each shape or arrangement? Which are the most common types?

(See copiable worksheet 4.2)

- Visit a garden centre and record all the shapes and types of leaves of plants. Where do these plants live naturally? Are their leaves like ones we can see growing around the school?
- Use a key to identify different types of leaves (the identification sheets in the pack *Action for plants* are very good – see Chapter 11 page 139 for details).
- Measure leaves on the sunny side of a tree or bush (south facing) and a shady side. Are the leaves bigger on one side than another? Why might this be?

Plants can be meat eaters

Children are fascinated by the fact that some plants can gobble up whole insects. It seems the stuff of science fiction. Remember, though, that these plants still have green parts so they must be photosynthesising. Most insectivorous plants live in boggy places where the acidic soil lacks nitrogen. Plants must have nitrogen to produce new growth. A meal of insects makes up for this deficiency and allows them to survive.

Figure 4.5 Examples of insectivorous plants

Venus flytrap

Pitcher plant

Sundew

See CD-ROM:
Insectivorous plants

The *Venus flytrap* is perhaps the most familiar example and can be obtained from garden centres and grown in schools (see section below). Its leaves are hinged and the trap is sprung when an insect touches trigger hairs inside the pair of leaves, causing massive and sudden expansion, pulling the leaves shut over the hapless victim. But why don't raindrops or particles touching these hairs result in false alarms? The trick seems to be that the trigger hairs must be touched twice before the leaf hinge is stimulated – clever!

Pitcher plants literally drown their victims. The smell of rotting meat is the attraction and as the insect investigates it slips into the deep, slippery-sided chamber filled with liquid which forms its death chamber. Even frogs have fallen victim to the larger varieties found in tropical forests.

Sundews are tiny plants with sticky fingers as leaves. The attraction this time is sugary nectar, but the shiny globules on each leaf hair are there to deceive. They are covered with a sticky glue ensnaring the insect. Other hairs on the sides of the leaf join in to hold the victim and then the whole leaf curls around the prey until digestive juices secreted by the leaf have done their work.

Growing and keeping insectivorous plants

Sundews and Venus flytrap are the varieties to grow. Grow plants in peat-based compost mixed with equal parts of vermiculite. Moisten the soil and keep it moist with rainwater or distilled or deionised water. NEVER USE TAP WATER. It contains lime which will kill them.

Figure 4.6 Growing plants in a propagator made from a plastic bottle

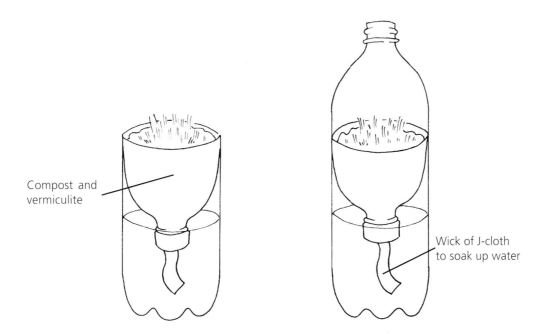

Compost and vermiculite

Wick of J-cloth to soak up water

A good way to keep insectivorous plants is to include them as part of an eco-column. This will also help to show children the interdependence of living things.

Instructions for making an eco-column can be found on the SAPS website at: http://www-saps.plantsci.cam.ac.uk/worksheets

Literacy links

Key Stage 2 Vocabulary

Alternate
Breathe
Chlorophyll
Insect
Opposite
Overlap
Pair
Photosynthesis
Pointed
Rosette
Single
Spiral
Tip
Tropical

Literacy-related activities	Most suitable for NC year
Encourage children to use a range of terms to describe how leaves are arranged on plants, e.g. rosette, alternate, opposite, paired, spiral, single.	Y4
Use a concept map to explore children's understanding of how plants make food. Use concept terms on labels such as *leaf, stem, root, plant, food, water, air, fertiliser,* and linking words or phrases such as, *is made in/by, enters, leaves, stored in, produced by.*	Y3–6
Can children follow instructions on the text of a worksheet? (see copiable worksheet 4.1)	Y5/6
Give the class a range of questions about plants and food, e.g. How does the leaf make food; what arrangement of leaves is most common; which leaves make most food? Ask groups of children to say which questions can be answered by carrying out a survey, investigating or seeking information from a book.	Y4/5

Text-related work

Fiction
Children could write a story entitled *Escape from the Jaws of Death*, based on the adventures of a fly who managed to escape the deadly Venus flytrap.

Non-fiction
Get children to research the ways in which insectivorous plants attract and trap insects – a number of sources could be used (see Chapter 11).

Numeracy and information and communications technology (ICT) links

Activities related to numeracy objectives	Objectives relevant to NC year
Survey plants and record angles at which leaves join the stem $\vdash$, $\vdash$ or $\vdash$. Get children to identify which pattern is most common.	Y3
Work out how much of the Sun's energy falling on grass gets into a beefburger.	Y4
Encourage children to categorise leaf arrangement using the correct names for these types of angles.	Y5
Trace leaf shapes onto squared paper and ask children to comment on the types of symmetry they can see.	Y3/4
Get children to identify the axis of symmetry for different leaf shapes. Is there a similar pattern for all leaves?	Y5
Get children to time how long it takes each leaf disc to rise in the experiment to measure rate of food making. Get them to work out an average time for leaf rise for different plants (see copiable worksheet 4.1).	Y5

ICT links	Relating to QCA unit
Get children to use a digital camera to record leaf shapes and leaf arrangements (or use images from the CD-ROM). Get them to paste these pictures under the correct categories and to add text for names of plants and the categories.	3A
Children could make branching databases (keys) using features and arrangements of leaves and yes/no alternatives.	4C

See CD-ROM:
Leaf forms

Measuring how fast a leaf makes food

As leaves make food they produce oxygen. In this experiment the rate at which the leaf makes oxygen is used to see how fast it makes food.

1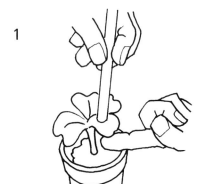

2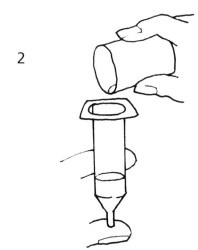

1. Cut out four leaf discs by pushing a plastic straw into a leaf.
2. Pull the plunger out of a plastic syringe and add 5ml of liquid. *Note to teacher – the syringes should be 5cm³ clear plastic and the liquid is made by adding 3.5 grams of bicarbonate of soda to 250cm³ of distilled water. Add one drop of washing up liquid to stop the leaf discs sticking to the sides of the syringe.*

3   BLOW

4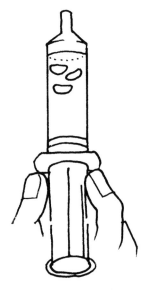

3. Gently blow the leaf discs into the liquid in the syringe.
4. Hold the syringe upright and put the plunger back into it.

5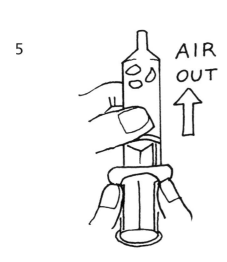

6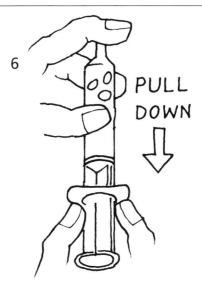

5. Push out all the air.

6. Put your finger over the open end of the syringe. Gently pull the plunger down. Bubbles should appear on the surface of the leaf discs.

7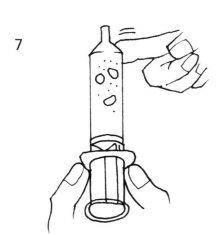

8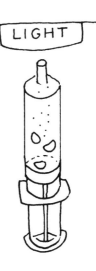

7. Tap the syringe to make all the leaf discs sink.

8. Put your syringe under a strong light or light bank. Time how long it takes each leaf disc to rise.

● Why did you have to suck all the air out of the discs in step 6?

● What made the leaf discs rise to the top? What was going on inside the leaf to make this happen?

● Would leaf discs rise if you put black paper around the syringe? Try it.

● What do you think will happen if you colour the syringe green?

● Try the experiment with leaf discs from ivy plants or from geranium plants. Do the discs rise as fast?

Copiable worksheet 4.2: Upper juniors

Looking at leaves

How many plants can you see with leaves arranged like this? Write the names of plants under each drawing.

Alternate

Opposite

Whorls

Rosette

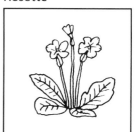

_____

_____

_____

● How many plants can you find with the leaf shapes shown below?

● If any leaves don't fit these groups think up your own types.

Compound leaflets

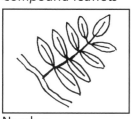

Number _____

Lobed

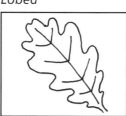

Number _____

Finger-like

Number _____

Oval – smooth edges

Number _____

Oval – toothed edges

Number _____

Heart shaped

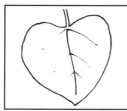

Number _____

Oval and long

Number _____

Nearly round

Number _____

Prickly

Number _____

Needles

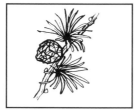

Number _____

Own type _____

Number _____

Own type _____

Number _____

Chapter 5

Water: a question of balance

ONE of the first things children say a plant needs is water. We all know what happens when plants don't get enough – those poor, drooping plants after the school holidays, or the hanging baskets at the end of a hot summer's day. As we saw in the last chapter, the taking up of materials from the ground dominates thinking about plants and the way they make food. We also learned that plants need some water to provide hydrogen to reduce carbon dioxide from air to make sugar, but they require a lot more of it for other reasons.

All living cells contain a material called *cytoplasm* and this is 80% water. Plant cells also have an extra watery sap held inside a sac or *vacuole* – so plants contain even more water than animals. A lettuce is 99% water.

National Curriculum links:
Key Stage 1: Sc2 3a.
Key Stage 2: Sc2 3c, 5c.

Links with units in the QCA scheme of work for science:
3B Helping plants grow well.
6A Interdependence and adaptation.

Figure 5.1 A typical plant cell

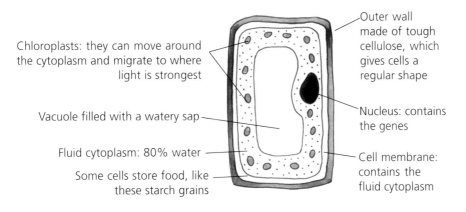

Chloroplasts: they can move around the cytoplasm and migrate to where light is strongest

Vacuole filled with a watery sap

Fluid cytoplasm: 80% water

Some cells store food, like these starch grains

Outer wall made of tough cellulose, which gives cells a regular shape

Nucleus: contains the genes

Cell membrane: contains the fluid cytoplasm

Trees and woody shrubs have strengthened tissues to hold them up, but most plants rely on the internal pressure of water in their cells. When these cells lose too much water, their stems and leaves cannot support themselves and the plant wilts.

Plants also need to take up water from their surroundings because it contains tiny amounts of chemicals needed for a healthy life. Magnesium and iron, for example, are essential components of the chlorophyll molecule, and a plant lacking these will often have yellow patches on its leaves.

Water is the medium in which biochemical activity takes place. The sugars and amino-acids needed for new growth and ripening of fruits must be carried around the plant in a liquid.

Getting to the top

See CD-ROM:
Ancient plants

You may know that the world's tallest plants, at some 60 metres, are reckoned to be the giant sequoia redwood trees of California. In the world of plant records, however, the great Australian mountain ash (actually a type of eucalyptus) beats this. A fallen trunk was once measured at 143 metres long and they regularly grow to over 92 metres. How does water get to the top leaves of these giants?

Figure 5.2 Giant redwood trees in California

You may remember a school physics experiment showing that air pressure can support a column of mercury to a height of 76cm. Now water is 13 times less dense than mercury, so this means that air pressure can support a height of water of about 10 metres (33 feet). This, according to physics, is the theoretical maximum height of a tree – but even our humble British trees regularly exceed this.

Therefore there must be other forces at work. In the last chapter we saw that leaves have pores in their lower surfaces, through which they take in carbon dioxide and lose oxygen. Water evaporates from the air spaces inside leaves and escapes through these same pores. As each molecule is lost to the air, another takes its place. The chain of water molecules goes right back through the leaf to the veins and all the way down through the stem, into the roots and eventually to the water in the soil. The evaporation of water from leaves is called *transpiration*, and the water chain the *transpiration stream*. The passage of water up the stem is helped by the fact that water molecules are stuck together by electrical forces. A helping hand is provided by the design of the plant's plumbing system. The *xylem* vessels that carry water from soil to leaf have ultra smooth insides and are very narrow. This helps water molecules to creep up inside them by a process called *capillary action*.

So for every molecule of water lost from a leaf, another takes its place. As long as there is enough water in the supply line, plants are not in danger.

Figure 5.3 Water uptake and loss in a plant

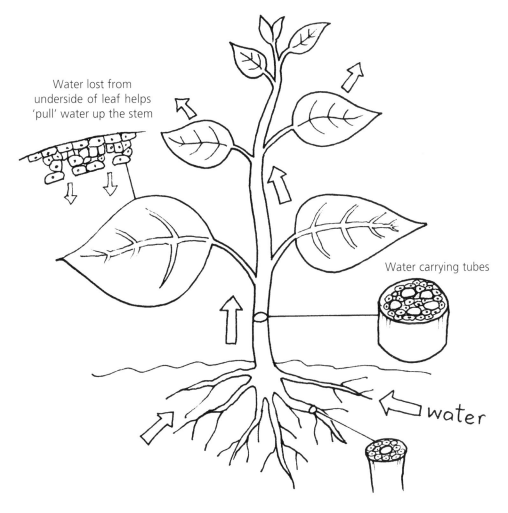

Water lost from underside of leaf helps 'pull' water up the stem

Water carrying tubes

water

Hollow tubes at root centre

Children's ideas about water and plants

- Children are likely to think that leaves soak up water.
- Children are generally unaware of the different ways in which plants use water.

Activities: Exploring water uptake and loss (KS2)

- Cover some leaves of a potted plant with a plastic bag. Look at your plant the next day. What do you notice inside the plastic bag? Plan an experiment to see if plants lose more water in the day than at night.
- Grow a rooted plant in a plastic bottle of water. Seal the top of the plastic bottle with cling film (why do you have to do this?).

Figure 5.4 Growing plants in bottles

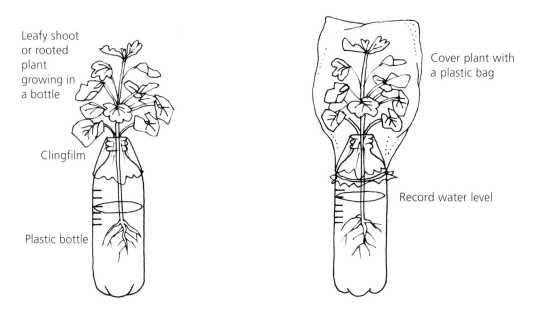

Leafy shoot or rooted plant growing in a bottle

Clingfilm

Plastic bottle

Cover plant with a plastic bag

Record water level

- Make marks on the bottle to see how much water the plant loses in a day or a week. Find out if the plant uses more or less water if you put a plastic bag over it or move it to a much warmer place.

David Bellamy, the famous TV botanist, has worked out that an oak tree loses about 107 litres of water every day.

- Find something that would hold this much water – a bath or bucket perhaps?
- How many buckets or baths of water would an oak tree lose in a week, month, year?
- Why might your figures not be very accurate (think about water loss throughout the year – see numeracy links section).
- Give children sticks of celery – preferably with leaves on. Cut off the bottom 5mm with a knife and ask them to put celery stalks into a cup of red ink solution (see copiable worksheet 5.1).

The next day children can look at the celery and its leaves. They can gently break the celery to reveal the plant plumbing system (now stained red). They can cut the stem across to see how far the colour goes.

For an extra special effect you can get a white flower – carnations or chrysanthemums are ideal. Carefully slit the stem with a sharp knife. Put each half of the cut stem into a different colour of ink – you should get a two-tone flower.

Life in the balance – how plants cope with water stress

The amount of water a plant takes up and loses is a fine balancing act. If plants don't draw up enough in the transpiration stream they are in trouble. But if loss exceeds supply, the problems are even worse. In dry places, like deserts and sand dunes, special design measures are the order of the day.

As water is lost from leaves, reducing the surface area of your leaves is one way to conserve what little water is on offer. Cacti have reduced their leaves to protective spines. The fleshy stem has become green, taking the role of photosynthesis from the leaves and storing water in special cells and spaces.

See CD-ROM:
Desert Plants

Figure 5.5 Desert plants

Coniferous trees have thin needles to cut down water loss – but why do they need to do this in a wet climate like Britain's? The answer lies in the fact that their ancestors grew after the ice age when water supplies remained frozen in the ground for much of the year. The great coniferous forests of Scandinavia, Canada and Russia still have to cope with this type of water stress.

See CD-ROM:
Ancient plants

See CD-ROM:
Dunes and marsh

Marram grass is one of the most important plants of sand dunes. Its extensive root system binds the shifting sands together preventing coastal erosion. Marram's solution to the lack of water is to tuck its *stomata* (the pores that let out the water) away deep inside hair-lined pits. The hairs and pits cut down air movement, so making the air moist around the pores – cutting down transpiration. As an added feature the whole leaf can roll up to cut water loss further.

Figure 5.6 A section across a rolled-up leaf of Marram grass

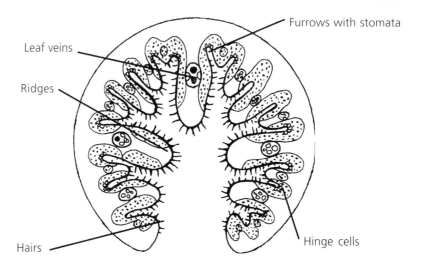

You would think that living in a marsh by the sea would present few problems for plants – after all, there is water all around. The problem is that it's salty. Plant roots have tiny hair-like cells, and these take in water only when the solution inside the cell vacuole has less water molecules than the surrounding soil or marsh. In other words, water molecules move from a dilute solution into a stronger one. Botanists call this process osmosis.

Copiable worksheet 5.2 has an activity that you can use to investigate this process.

Marsh plants have special sap packed with salts so that they can reverse the tendency of water to be sucked out of their roots into the salty marsh. Their leaves and stems are often fleshy and packed with mucilage, a substance that retains water. Samphire grows wild in the mudflats and creeks of the north Norfolk coast. The young, tender shoots are often picked and eaten with a little butter before they get too salty. The adult plant is so packed with salts that it used to be harvested and refined as a source of salt for glassmaking – hence its other name, *glasswort*.

Too much of a good thing

We have already seen that being surrounded by salty water causes osmotic problems. Plants living permanently soaked in water have other things to worry about. Firstly they must avoid rotting. The cedars growing in the Louisiana swamps near New Orleans are constructed of particularly tough rot-resistant timber.

Another problem is suffocation. Roots like other parts of the plant must respire and to do this they must get access to oxygen. One solution is to sprout roots above ground to breathe fresh air. These special roots are called 'knees', and you can see them in the photograph of the mangrove plants shown below.

Figure 5.7 Cedar trees growing in a Louisiana swamp near New Orleans

See CD-ROM:
Swamps

Figure 5.8 The mangrove plant has special aerial roots called 'knees'

Living in the rain soaked forests of the tropics causes special problems for leaves. Plants living under the canopy get a regular soaking every day from the deluge of rain falling onto them from vegetation above.

Have you ever noticed something in common when you look at many of the exotic plants sold in supermarkets? They all have leaves with elongated points called 'drip tips'.

See CD-ROM:
Leaf forms

Figure 5.9 Typical rainforest plants showing leaves with 'drip tips'

These tips channel rain away from the leaf very fast. The overall shape of leaves and their shiny upper skins also help to shift water so that the leaves do not get waterlogged.

Activities: Comparing leaves

- Get children to look at leaves of tropical houseplants and compare the shapes of leaves with shapes of common British plants. How many plants have 'drip tips'?

This could be carried out on a visit to the hothouse of a botanical garden (see Chapter 11 page 149).

- Investigate the rate at which water drains off leaves with 'drip tips' compared with other shapes (see copiable worksheet 5.3).

Literacy links

Key Stage 2 Vocabulary

Cactus
Cells
Desert
Evaporation
Rainforest
Rate
Salt
Wilt

Literacy-related activities	Most suitable for NC year
Get children to plan the steps to carry out an investigation: Will a plant lose more water at night than during the day? Which leaf shapes does water drain fastest from?	Y2–5
Use a 'planning flower' (see Chapter 10 on Progression and copiable sheet 10.1) to help structure children's plans. Encourage them to write a plan using openers and connections, e.g. First I will . . . then I shall . . . To keep my test fair I will . . . I will record my results by . . .	Y2–5

Numeracy links

Activities related to numeracy objectives	Objectives relevant to NC year
Find a container that holds 1 litre, 2 litres, 5 litres, 10 litres. Compare these sizes to show how much water a plant like an oak tree might lose in a day in summer.	Y2
Work out how much water an oak tree would lose in a week, month and year (assuming that it loses 100 litres in a day – 24 hours).	Y3/4
Record how quickly colouring rises up a celery stalk (see copiable worksheet 5.1). Work out (from a graph) whether colour rises faster up the bottom half of the stalk than it does up the upper half.	Y5/6
Use results from the potato chip experiment (see copiable worksheet 5.2) to calculate the percentage of weight lost or gained by the chips.	Y5/6

Drink up

Cut the end off a stick of celery. CAREFUL WITH KNIVES! Get your teacher to help you do this.

- Put the cut end into a cup of coloured water.

- Look at your celery every ten minutes. What has happened?

_____

_____

- Measure with a ruler how far the water goes up the stick after each 10 minutes.

- Record your results in this table:

Time in minutes	How far red ink has travelled in centimetres (cm)
10	
20	
30	
40	
50	
60	

Your teacher may help you to draw a graph of your results or you could use a computer to help you.

Copiable worksheet 5.1 *continued*

- Did the coloured water travel fastest up the celery at the beginning or towards the end of the experiment? How can you tell from your results?

_____

_____

When you have finished your experiment, bend your celery stick until it begins to break and have a look inside it.

- What can you see?

_____

_____

- Pull out the coloured 'strands'. What do these 'strands' or tubes do for the plant?

_____

_____

Swelling and shrinking chips

1. Peel some potatoes and cut them into chips. TAKE CARE WITH KNIVES!

2. Divide the chips into two piles.

 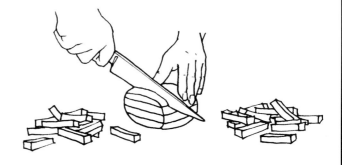

3. Dry the chips with kitchen towel.

4. Weigh each pile of chips and write the results in the table shown overleaf.

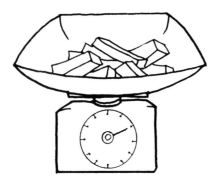 

5. Put one pile of chips into a bowl of ordinary water and the other pile into a bowl of salty water.

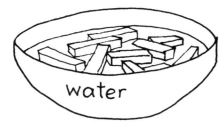 

6. After about 40 minutes, take each pile of chips out of the water and dry them with kitchen towel.

7. Weigh each set of chips again and put the results into the table shown below.

8. Work out how much weight each pile of chips has lost or gained.

9. Feel the chips. How do they feel compared with the chips at the start?

Results

	A	B	C		
	Weight of chips at the start	Weight of chips at the end	Loss (-) or gain (+) in weight [(A) minus (B)]	Loss (-) or gain(+) in weight as a percentage (%) [(C) divided by (A) x 100]	Feel of the chips at the end
Chips in plain water					
Chips in salty water					

Now answer these questions about your experiment.

● How have the chips from each bowl changed?

● What has happened to make the chips change in weight?

● Has water gone into the potato chips or has it come out of them? How can you tell from your results?

● Why do plants have problems if they live in places where the soil is salty?

● Think of some places where the surroundings of plants are salty.

Copiable worksheet 5.3: Lower juniors

Drip-dry leaves

1. Draw an outline of a *rainforest leaf* onto card or
   paper and cut out your leaf shape.

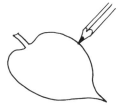

2. Draw an outline of a *British woodland leaf* onto card
   or paper and cut out your leaf shape. Make it about the
   same size as the rainforest leaf.

3. Make two leaf 'midribs' and 'veins' from garden wire. Press these onto
   some sticky-backed plastic.

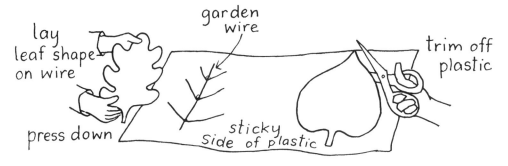

4. Press your card leaves down onto the sticky-backed plastic. Trim off the
   plastic so that you have a nice leaf model.

5. Paint your 'British woodland' leaf with PVA glue and sprinkle sand onto
   it. This is because woodland leaves are often rough and hairy.

6. Do not paint the rainforest leaf.

Now you can test your leaves to see how much water drains from their
surfaces. You could do this by seeing how much of a cupfull of water can
be collected in a certain time.

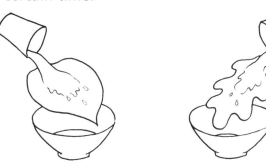

How will you make your tests fair?

Test each side of your leaves to see if more or less water can be collected.

Chapter 6

Carrying on

SOME scientists promote the idea that living things have one sole purpose in life – to ensure the continuation of their genes. Plants have invested millions of years of evolutionary effort devising a huge range of techniques to ensure they do this.

In this chapter we take a look at some of the ways flowers are designed to 'get laid' – not forgetting that many of them 'do it' on the wind. We also look at how plants get the results of all this sex to new places so that their genes can exploit new opportunities.

National Curriculum links:
Key Stage 1: Sc2 3a, 3b, 4b.
Key Stage 2: Sc2 1b, 3d, 4b, 4c.

Links with units in the QCA scheme of work for science:
2B Plants and animals in the local environment.
2C Variation
5B Life cycles.

An attractive business

'Beauty is in the eye of the beholder', as they say. For many flowering plants this means putting on an attractive display of colour and smell to exploit the senses of pollinators. The purpose is to lure the animal to the flower, get it to crawl down towards some sweet (or foul) smelling part deep inside, brush against ripe pollen sacks which shower the creature with pollen grains (the male sex cells), and then rely on this pollen being stuck to the stigma of the next flower visited. In this country, insects like bees, flies, hoverflies, butterflies and moths visit flowers. But in the tropics birds, bats and even land mammals like the Australian honey possum can get in on the act.

Figure 6.1 A bee pollinating a dandelion flower

Photograph courtesy of Action for Plants (Tate & Lyle)

The diagram below shows the working parts of a flower. All parts of a flower are evolved from modified leaves. Poinsettia, often given as a gift at Christmas, has red-coloured leaf bracts rather than petals to form its flower.

Figure 6.2 A cross-section through a flower showing the parts

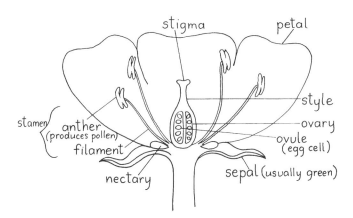

Sepals are the remains of green scale leaves that protected the flower in bud. *Petals* are there to attract the pollinators and are often formed into a tube so that insects have to crawl down towards the sweet-smelling *nectaries*. Some petals are formed into shapes to mimic another insect, like the flower of the bee orchid. Insects can see into the ultraviolet end of the spectrum and many flowers, particularly white and blue varieties, have bold lines guiding insects towards nectaries. We can only see these when an ultraviolet light is shone onto them. The spots on foxglove petals also attract bees. Flowers like deadnettles have special landing platforms for insects. The platform is perfectly balanced so that, when a bee lands on it, the anthers are pulled onto the bee's hairy back showering it with pollen.

Figure 6.3 A variety of flower shapes

See CD-ROM: *Flowers*

Tropical rainforest orchid

Foxglove

Hibiscus

The male sex cells of a plant are its pollen grains – the equivalent of sperm in animals. The grains are produced and held inside the pollen sacs of *anthers*. These structures are timed to ripen and split just at the right moment, usually before the female parts of the same flower are ripe, to avoid the flower having sex with itself. The anthers are held on *filaments* attached to petals or the base of the flower. The whole male structure of filament and anther is referred to as the *stamen*.

The female parts are at the centre of the flower. The *stigma* is at the tip of the female organs and is ridged and grooved, perfectly matching the shape of pollen arriving from the same species. The match is not just physical. The pollen of each plant carries a unique chemical signature checked by the stigma.

After the pollen grain's credentials have been checked and accepted, it can begin its task. A sugary solution on the stigma stimulates the growth of a pollen tube and this grows down through the fleshy tissues of the *style*, until the female sex cell or *ovule*, held inside an *ovary*, is reached. The final act is the moment of fertilisation, when the pollen grain's nucleus finally fuses with the ovule's nucleus and their genes mix.

Figure 6.4 Diagram showing the growth of a pollen tube

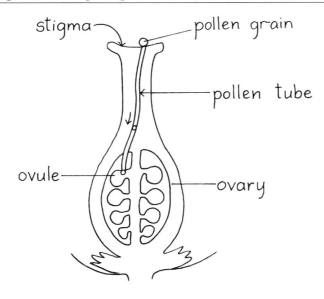

Children's ideas about plant reproduction and life cycles

- Most children think that flowers are always brightly coloured. Few children realise that grasses have flowers.
- Some children think that petals protect the flower.
- Young children often think that all plants die in winter.
- Children (and many adults) use only the greengrocer's term for fruit – a sweet-tasting and fleshy fruiting body.

To the botanist, all structures containing seeds are fruits, and so nuts, pea-pods, tomatoes, peppers and cucumbers are included.

On the wind

We saw in the second chapter that plants without brightly coloured, large flowers are rarely regarded as true plants by children. They are genuinely surprised, for example, to learn that grasses have flowers.

Depending on the wind to carry your genes from one flower to another seems a risky business compared with employing animals to do the job. To ensure maximum success, wind-pollinated flowers have small, insignificant petals that allow large anthers to hang outside the flowers, dangling in the wind.

Figure 6.5 A drawing showing the floret of perennial rye grass

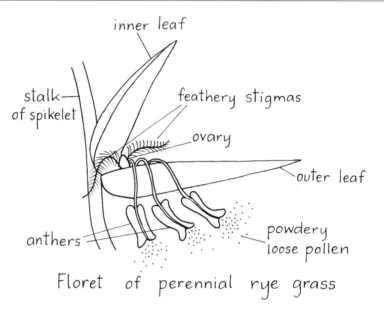

The pollen is produced in vast amounts. Grains are small and light so they can float for miles even on a light breeze. Hayfever sufferers curse the huge production of grass pollen as these plants ripen in June and July. Stigmas are feathery and hang right outside the petals like a net to catch pollen drifting past them.

Activities: Flowers (KS1 and 2)

Survey different types of flowers around the school, from gardens or from shops.

- Count the numbers of petals on each flower. Record how many flowers have four, five, six or more than six petals. Look in books to find plant families defined by the numbers of petals on their flowers (see copiable worksheet 6.1).

Collect a variety of different flowers – large varieties from gardens and shops are best.

- Ask children to make 'flower cards' – like the one shown below – by carefully pulling off the different parts and sticking them onto white card with sticky tape (KS2).

Figure 6.6 An example of a flower card

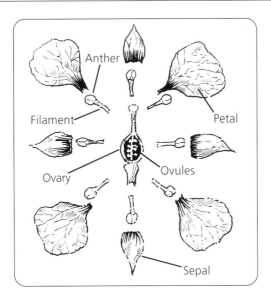

- Make a datafile or display of flower cards. Look in books to see what families flowers belong to. Add information from books, etc. See copiable worksheet 6.2).
- Make a card or paper model flower to show all the working parts (see copiable worksheet 6.3).
- Make a model flower from plastic bottles and other materials.

See CD-ROM:
Plant activities

Figure 6.7 A model flower

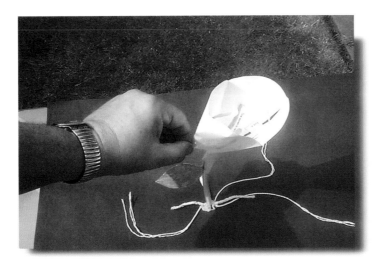

The instructions for making a plastic bottle flower model can be found on the SAPS website – see Chapter 11 page 145.

Going without

Many plants can produce new offspring without sex. The disadvantage is that the new offspring will be genetically identical to their parents – there has been no mixing of genes. Any deficiencies or malformations will be continued. This is why most plants using *vegetative propagation,* as it is officially called, use flowers for reproduction as well. The flowers do not carry on the genes – the seeds do!

See CD-ROM:
Use of plants

Many of the examples we can show children are common food plants, as humans have regularly exploited this ability of plants. Potatoes are produced as fleshy *tubers* on underground parts of the stem (not as part of the roots – as most people think). The ginger plant produces a stout underground stem – a *rhizome*. Onions, like daffodils, are *bulbs* – the swollen bases of leaves.

Some plants produce a number of thin side branches radiating from the main plant like spokes of a wheel. The strawberry produces *runners* bearing a number of buds or nodes. Where each node touches the moist earth, rootlets sprout and eventually a new strawberry plant grows. Very soon, from just a few parent plants, you will have a whole strawberry patch for free.

The spider plant (common as a houseplant and easy to grow in school) bears its offspring at the end of stalks called *stolons.*

Activities: Vegetative propagation (KS1 and 2)

Figure 6.8 An amaryllis flower

See CD-ROM:
Spring flowers and bulbs

Amaryllis is a large and spectacular bulb that can be bought between January and April. Following its development and growth is a good way for children to follow the life cycle of a plant.

- Plant an amaryllis bulb and record all the changes as it grows and flowers. Chart its growth by cutting out pieces of paper the same height as the stem and sticking them onto a growth chart every three days until it stops growing.

- Get children to collect small strawberry plants from runners, or 'baby' spider plants from the end of their stolons, and plant them into new pots.
- Cut the tops from carrots, parsnips and swedes and sprout them in saucers of water. Cover the saucers with the top half of a plastic bottle to stop the water evaporating.

Figure 6.9 Some examples of common vegetative organs

See CD-ROM:
Plant activities

Spreading out

One of the real successes of plants is their ability to colonise and exploit available space. When the virgin rock of Sertsey Island erupted out of the seas off Iceland in the 1960s, it was only a matter of months before a variety of plants arrived on the scene.

When the ovule has been fertilised by the pollen cell's nucleus an embryo plant develops surrounded by a store of food and a protective coat – the seed (see Chapter 3). The remaining part of the ovary either swells with sugary tissue and ripens, or hardens to form a pod or nut-like structure. In both cases these are properly called *fruits*. To a botanist, a fruit is merely the capsule in which a plant contains its seed ready for distribution rather than the term we normally use for the sweet and fleshy varieties that we eat (see children's ideas section above).

The variety of clever ways in which plants get their seeds to new places is truly awesome. The oak is a minimalist in this game. Its acorns simply fall from the hard lower case of the fruit onto the ground. This might not seem like a good idea, since new trees are hardly likely to succeed under the spreading canopy of the parent. The trick is that the parent oak inhibits new growth within range of its own roots by chemical means. The oak must rely on birds foraging for nuts or on forgetful squirrels to carry its offspring some distance away, and with these simple strategies it seems to have been successful.

Figure 6.10 Acorns are distributed by animals

Photograph courtesy of
Action for Plants (Tate & Lyle)

Animals can also be employed as passive carriers. The seeds of burdock have perfectly-designed hooks that lock onto the furry coats of mammals (and people – see Chapter 9). The design is so impressive that it provided the inventor of Velcro with the idea for a new product. Many other plants produce bright, juicy, sweet berries, which encourages animals to eat their fruits. The seeds surviving digestion are then dropped in a nice dollop of fertiliser onto new ground.

Many plants with hard fruits have concentrated on designs for flight. The weight of each sycamore seed is so perfectly counterbalanced by its winged fruit that it can travel for great distances, spiralling gently like a helicopter on even light breezes. The fruits of dandelion and rosebay willow herb have tufts of silky hairs and float like parachutes. On summer days it can seem as if the air is full of such tufted seeds.

See CD-ROM:
Flowers

Figure 6.11 Dandelion seed head

Plants with pods go for explosive distribution. The sides of broom pods facing the sun dry faster than sides in shade, and this sets up enormous tensions within the fruit, finally resulting in an explosion that flings the seeds far from the parent.

One long distance traveller that is now easy to show to children (supermarkets and garden centres regularly sell germinated examples quite cheaply) is the coconut. Coconut palms grow close to coasts and their fruit is a perfect package for long distance travel by sea. A hairy outer coat, able to trap air, adds buoyancy, and the coconut flesh and milk provide ample rich food for the germinating seed when an island or coast is reached.

Figure 6.12 Seeds dispersed by explosion of pods or fruit

Brazil nut fruit   Devil's claw   Squirting cucumber

Photograph courtesy of Action for Plants (Tate & Lyle)

Activities (KS1 & 2)

- Collect a number of varieties of seeds in their fruiting bodies (please check with *Be Safe* – see Chapter 11, page 140 – as some seeds and fruits can be harmful if eaten, e.g. lupin seeds). Ask children to say how the examples might be spread.

Suitable examples are: sycamore, acorns (in their cups), rosebay willow herb, heads of poppies, burdock and cleavers, soft fruits such as blackcurrant, elderberry and strawberry, true berries such as grapes, and fruits with a single stone such as nectarines, peaches and plums.

- Display a range of fruits including vegetable types such as courgettes, aubergines, melons, tomatoes, peas, mangetouts and nuts in their cases (N.B. check for any known nut allergies in the class) (KS1).
- Show children examples of fruits commonly included in diets and celebrations in other cultures – see Chapter 9 for ideas and activities (KS1/2).
- Investigate a number of wind dispersed fruits dropped from a standard height. Put marks on the floor where they land. Measure the distances and calculate an average for each plant tested. Which plant was most successful? (See copiable worksheet 6.4)

Literacy links

Vocabulary

Key Stage 1	Key Stage 2
Bud	Anther
Fruit	Disperse
Petal	Fertilise
Seed	Nectary
Spread	Ovary
	Pollen
	Pollinate
	Stamen
	Stigma

Literacy-related activities	Most suitable for NC year
Look at pictures/photographs of plants and sequence into spring, summer, autumn and winter. Put *labels* with these words next to pictures.	R/Y1
Sequence pictures showing the stages in the life cycle of a plant and add *captions* to show what is happening at each.	Y2/3
Label parts of a flower (*petal*, *sepal*, *anther*, *stamen*) with pre-prepared or own labels. Add captions saying what each part does.	Y4/5
Make non-fiction booklets giving information about different plants and how they reproduce, e.g. by *flowers*, *tubers*, *runners*, *underground stems*, *bulbs*. Children could do the same for types of fruits or methods of seed dispersal. Add pictures, photographs and information *researched from texts* using *indexes* in information books and encyclopaedias.	Y4–6

Text-related work

Fiction
Read classic children's poems describing and celebrating flowers and flower structure/beauty – see Chapter 11 page 144 for examples (KS1, KS2).

Give children a poem that describes parts of a flower and ask children to reflect on it (shared text work). Ask children if any of the parts of the story of pollination are missing. Ask children to write their own poems based on parts of the flower – see Rosemary Feasey's book *Primary Science and Literacy Links* pages 41 and 93 – Chapter 11 page 140 gives details (KS2).

There are a number of stories that can also link with work on flowers, seasonal change and seed dispersal, for example Roald Dahl's book *James and the Giant Peach* – see Chapter 11 page 142 for suggestions (KS1, KS2).

Non-fiction
Encourage the use of identification guides, e.g. simple field guides describing types of flowers. This will help children to see how keys are used in books to relate types of information. Examples of suitable books are given in Chapter 11 (KS2).

Numeracy and information and communications technology (ICT) links

Activities related to numeracy objectives	Objectives relevant to NC year
Count how many flowers have four, five, six and more than six petals. Children could do this on a trip around the school or from a collection of flowers in a super-market or from a shop – even imitation flowers will do. (See copiable worksheet 6.1)	Y1/2
Draw a pictograph of the results above.	Y2
Record distances for seeds to travel when they are dropped from the same height. Calculate an average distance travelled for each seed. (See copiable worksheet 6.4.)	Y4
Record flower symmetry by tracing or copying (see below) flower shapes (many flowers have radial symmetry but some have bilateral or reflective symmetry). Look for repeated patterns in flowers, e.g. arrangements of petals in flowers with separate whorls – spiral/concentric arrangement of flower parts.	Y4/5

ICT links	Relating to QCA unit
Use a graphing program, e.g. *My World* or *Survey* (see Chapter 11 page 147), to draw a pictograph showing numbers of flowers of different colours or number of petals.	1E
Look at different types of flower. Create a datafile for each flower type recording numbers of petals, sepals, stamens, symmetry, colour, as well as information researched from texts, e.g. how long this plant flowers for, local traditions and uses, and the name of the flower family that it belongs to.	3C
Children could add digital or scanned photographs or their own drawings to the database above or use images from the CD-ROM.	3A
Place flowers onto a photocopier and copy shapes for analysis of symmetry.	
Use a word processor and/or DTP package to produce non-fiction pages as shown in the literacy links section.	

See CD-ROM:
Flowers

Copiable worksheet 6.1: Infants and lower juniors

Flowers

Look at flowers.

● Record how many flowers have different numbers of petals in the boxes below.

● Write down the different colours you see.

Four petals

Number of flowers with four petals

Colours _____

Five petals

Number of flowers with five petals

Colours _____

Six petals

Number of flowers with six petals

Colours _____

More than six petals

Number of flowers with more than six petals

Colours _____

Flowers with bell or tube shapes

Number of flowers with bell or tube shapes

Colours _____

● Which number of petals is the most common?

_____

● Which colour is the most common?

_____

Copiable worksheet 6.2: Lower and upper juniors

Flower data card

Stick the parts of the flower into the boxes below and cover them with clear plastic tape.

Flower name _____ Flower family _____

Habitat _____ Flowers from (month) _____ until (month) _____

Sepals _____

Number _____

Colour _____

Petals _____

Number _____

Colour _____

Stamens (male parts) _____

Number _____

Stigmas and ovaries *(female parts)* _____

Number _____

(Note: enlarge this sheet to A3 for larger flowers.)

Copiable worksheet 6.3: Lower and upper juniors

Making a model flower

Enlarge this sheet to A3.

Colour in the parts so that they look like a flower you have seen before you cut out your flower. Cut, glue and stick together as shown.

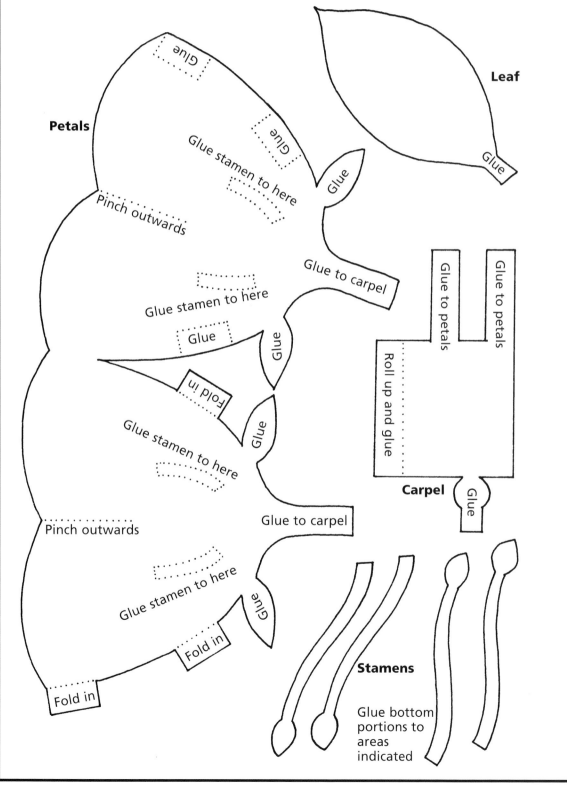

Which seed goes the furthest?

Good seeds to use for this are: a dandelion seed, a rosebay willow herb seed, an ash tree seed and a sycamore tree seed.

1. Predict which seeds will travel furthest when you drop them. Give reasons for your predictions.

2. Spread a sheet of paper on the floor and mark a cross in the centre.

3. Take each seed and hold it out so it is directly over the cross on the paper, as shown in the drawing below.

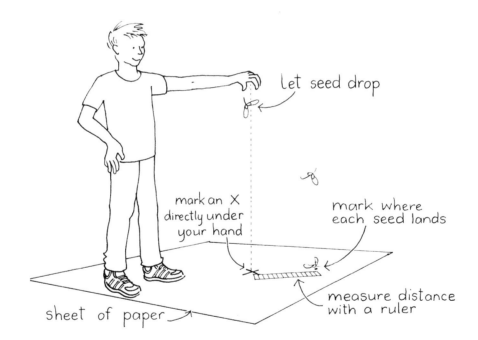

4. Have one of your group ready with a stopwatch.

5. Let the seed go and time how long it takes to fall.

6. Mark where the seed hits the ground and measure the distance from the cross on the paper with a tape measure.

Copiable worksheet 6.4 *continued*

7. Put your results into a table like this:

Seed tested	Time seed took to reach the ground in seconds	Distance seed travelled from the cross in cm

8. How do your results compare with your predictions?

9. Why did some seeds travel further? Was there a link between how far they went and how long they took to fall?

10. How would your results be different if you tried this investigation outside?

11. Try a conker (horse chestnut tree seed) or an acorn (from an oak tree). How far do they travel?

12. Why do plants try to get their seeds to travel away from the parent plant?

13. Wind can carry seeds away from a plant. What other methods of dispersal do plants use?

Chapter 7

Plants and the environment

PLANTS ARE the producers, directly or indirectly fuelling all other life. Since they occupy this fundamental position, it is not surprising that plant communities define the ecosystems found around the globe. We talk about the savannah grasslands of Africa, the tropical rainforests of South America and, closer to home, the moors of upland Britain. Each is defined by the unique community of plant types found there and this in turn shapes the topography, the look and feel of the environment, as well as determining what animals are found.

The environment is best explored directly, but this isn't easy if your school is surrounded by urban sprawl. There is much that can be done, however, using good stimulus materials, outside agencies and visits. Plants can survive almost anywhere, and even the most barren-looking playing field, tarmac playground or wall can provide a habitat for study.

Living together: plant communities

We think of a community in human terms as the people, jobs, houses, transport, and infrastructure of the modern world that affect the way we live and relate to each other at a local level. For an ecologist, a plant *community* means the collection of plants growing in a particular place that typifies a certain habitat. At the global level, plant communities are determined mainly by rainfall and temperature and are described as *biomes* covering huge areas of the Earth's surface. The coniferous forests of cool northern latitudes, the frozen Arctic tundra, the dry hot deserts and Mediterranean scrub are good examples. The plants that dominate these biomes have fine-tuned their photosynthesis to the climate. Spruce trees of the northern coniferous forests, for example, make most sugars at 18°C, while the acacia trees of the African savannah reach optimum productivity at 37°C.

At a local level, community types are more varied and their distribution is often determined by microclimate and altitude. The sunny, warm, southern slopes of a mountain will support woodland to a higher level than the colder more exposed northern slopes dominated by grassland, scrub and alpine tundra. The biome of Britain is *mixed deciduous woodland* and, centuries ago, much of the land was covered by forest.

National Curriculum links:
Key Stage 1: Sc2 1c, 5a, 5b, 5c.
Key Stage 2: Sc2 1c, 5a, 5b, 5c, 5d, 5e.

PSHE guidelines:
Key Stage 1: Ways in which people look after and improve environments.
Key Stage 2: Economic choices and sustainability. Looking after the school's environment.

Links with units in the QCA scheme of work for science:
2B Plants and animals in the local environment.
4B Habitats.
6 Interdependence and adaptation.
5/6H Enquiry in environmental and technological contexts.

See CD-ROM:
Habitats and Swamps

Figure 7.1 Example of plant biomes

Long grass savannah

Mangrove swamp in Florida

Today a wide variety of communities exists, each typified by collections of plants adapted to the specific microclimates, soil and rock features and the nutrients available. Human influence cannot be ignored. Much of the chalk grassland of southern England and the Pennines came about because the woods were cleared to make way for grazing animals like sheep and cattle. These animals and rabbits nibbled the woody herbs and shrubs, keeping the forest at bay. This fragile balance was upset with the near annihilation of the rabbit population by myxomatosis in the 1950s. Woodland returned, threatening this diverse grassland rich in rare lime-loving plants.

Figure 7.2 Typical British types

Sand dunes

Wet fenland

Heather moorland

See CD-ROM:
*Habitats and Dunes
and marsh*

In some communities one or two types of plants dominate. Upland moors are carpeted by heather or ling. Where two or more plants share the same ecological needs, competition occurs. At ground level in grassland this can reduce the diversity of species that co-exist. In a woodland, diversity is much higher because the community is *stratified*. The main competition in woods is for what light can penetrate the canopy of tree leaves above. Plants have evolved to occupy different levels in the wood, trapping what light they can. Woodland plants have phased their germination, growth and flowering throughout the spring and summer months to reduce competition for scarce resources.

Figure 7.3 The different layers of a woodland habitat

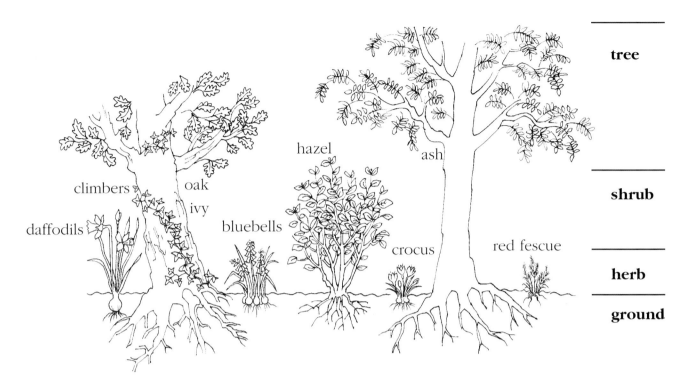

Different woods have different community structures. Birch trees produce an open canopy, so ground and herb layers are luxuriant and diverse. Beech trees have a dense canopy of leaves, all lying in the same direction, virtually blocking out the sun. Light falling on the woodland floor is minimal – not much can grow here once the canopy is established.

Figure 7.4 Different woodland canopy types

See CD-ROM:
Woodlands

Open canopy of a birch wood

The denser habitat of a pine wood

Activities: Surveying plant communities (KS2)

● Find out what plants make up communities in various places around the school.

Make a quadrat from an old coathanger made into a square. Get children to place the quadrat four times in each area and count the number of plants of each type.

Children should record their results using a tally system in a table (shown below). They could use simple guides to flowers, or photocopies, either of outline drawings showing the shapes of leaves, or taken from real leaves placed directly onto the photocopier (see Chapter 11 page 138 for examples).

| Name of plant | Places surveyed | | | | |
	cracks and crevices	football pitch	next to path	front lawn	freshly dug soil
Shepherd's purse	|||				||
Moss	ЖЖ		|||	ЖЖ ||	
Daisy	||	ЖЖ ЖЖ |||	ЖЖ ||	ЖЖ ЖЖ ЖЖ	
Plantain			||	ЖЖ		||	
Clover		||||	||	ЖЖ |||	||

● Investigate the occurrence of different plants across a path, or from the top to the bottom of a bank, or from the base of a hedge to the edge of a verge (see copiable worksheet 7.2).

Stretch out a line of string or tape to mark out a *transect* across the area to be studied, and get the children to place their wire quadrats every 2 metres along this line. Ask the children to record how much of their quadrat is covered by a particular plant. They could record their results using an abundance scale. For example:

1 = less than 1% of the quadrat is covered by the plant;
2 = between 1% and 5% of the quadrat is covered by the plant;
3 = between 5% and 25% of the quadrat is covered by the plant;
4 = between 25% and 50% of the quadrat is covered by the plant;
5 = between 50% and 75% of the quadrat is covered by the plant;
6 = between 75% and 100% of the quadrat is covered by the plant.

Record the results of the survey as a bar graph.

You could relate the results to the amount of water in the soil. Cheap water meters can be obtained from garden centres. They are just pushed into the soil to take a reading of moisture content.

Figure 7.5 Moisture meters

See CD-ROM:
Plant activities

- Make and colour in a chart, like the one below, to record flowering periods for different plants in a woodland or seen in the school grounds.

Flower	Jan	Feb	Mar	Apr	May	Jun	Jul	Aug	Sep	Oct	Nov	Dec
Daffodil												
Bluebell												
Crocus												
Dandelion												
Daisy												
Buttercup												

The weed species found in school grounds are fierce competitors and have evolved a number of features that allow them to survive. Plantain, daisies and dandelions all have tight rosettes of leaves close to the ground allowing them to grab maximum sunlight. Flowering buds and growing points are close to the ground so they are not destroyed by mowing. The leaves of plantain are particularly tough and this allows them to survive attack by slugs as well as trampling by children's feet.

See CD-ROM:
Leaf forms

Figure 7.6 Plants with rosettes of leaves growing amongst grass

Activities: Comparing habitats (KS1 and KS2)

See CD-ROM:
Habitats

Give children a number of A4-sized drawings of different habitats or communities, e.g. moorland, seashore, deciduous woodland, pond or wetland, desert, and a set of photographs or drawings of plants and animals that might live there.

- Ask children to match plants and animals with their correct habitats and to justify their choices. (Make sure that children have as many plants as animals to match up – see the section on children's ideas on page 90.)
- Make a display showing the different layers of a wood (see Figure 7.3 on page 83).
- Ask children to place animals and plants onto the display in their right places.
- Put question cards on the display and link questions to any visits the children have made: What did we see? What did we hear? What animals live in the tops of trees, in the ground layer, in the leaf litter, in holes in trees?
- Change the display to a night-time scene – now put in animals that would come out at night.

If you are visiting woodland:

- Go to different areas of the wood dominated by different types of tree. Measure the amount of light with a light meter or probe or by raising a PE hoop above your head and estimating how much of the sky you can see (KS2).

Record the types of plants and the percentage covered by ground and herb layers (KS2).

- Compare the numbers of minibeasts in the leaf litter underneath various types of trees (KS1 and 2).

You might find that the greatest diversity of minibeasts is associated with deep layers of soft leaves that decay easily, e.g. oak or beech. There are far fewer minibeasts amongst the dry hard leaf litter under beeches or in the acid environment of pine needles carpeting a coniferous wood.

Conservation

We have seen that a number of biomes of different plant communities exist across the globe. These communities represent the stable situation or *climax* of vegetation that is best adapted to local conditions. If this climax is disturbed or removed, it will try to re-establish itself. A disused piece of ground will go through a succession with competitive pioneer species, such as grasses and weeds succeeded by grassland and scrub, then by open copse and finally by full deciduous woodland. If the school pond is not managed, the water plants at the edge and on the banks will invade the water, and silt and mud will fill the pond until it succeeds to marsh, eventually to scrub and finally woodland.

In some cases the climax vegetation might be removed by drastic events. Heather moor produces a lot of dead material and, if this accumulates over a number of years, fires started naturally or due to human activity will burn so fiercely that roots and shoots are destroyed. The burned and exposed soil easily succeeds to scrub rather than moor. This is why good moorland management involves the selective burning of patches of moor on a yearly rotation to encourage strong new growth and avoid the dangers of destructive 'burn outs'.

See CD-ROM:
Habitats

In a way, conservation is about stopping succession in its tracks, and requires managing an area to maintain and preserve the diversity of the plant communities and their particular features that exist at any given time. It is sometimes necessary to protect habitats from human actions that disturb the delicate balance of their ecology. The table below shows some examples of plant communities and the typical management involved in their conservation.

See CD-ROM:
Conservation

Plant community/habitat	Common conservation management actions
Deciduous woodland	Thinning out trees and creating glades to allow a greater diversity of herb and ground-layer plants to develop. Cutting out invasive species such as sycamore.
Ponds, ditches and canals See CD-ROM: *Conservation and Habitats*	Cutting back emergent and marginal plants such as reeds, yellow flag iris and bullrush. Dredging to prevent silting up. Removing dense mats of submerged vegetation.
Sand dunes See CD-ROM: *Dunes and marsh*	Managing tracks to prevent people damaging the delicate dune system which can lead to 'blow outs', where wind erosion rips out the marram grass binding the dune together.
Mountains – alpine tundra and grass cover	Creating paved paths and walkways to prevent damage to plants that have taken hundreds of years to develop.
Flower meadow	Mowing timed to take place in late June or early July after wild flowers have set seed. Mowing should be height controlled so that shoots of ground-layer plants are not damaged.
Wet heath and bog	Controlling drainage to prevent drying out and succession to scrub or woodland and creation of boardwalks above fragile vegetation.

See CD-ROM: *Conservation*

Of course, conservation can also mean enhancement and improvement of land that was previously degraded by urbanisation or industrialisation. There have been some spectacular schemes, for example the landscaping and regeneration of former coal mines.

Development is not always bad. The building of motorways may be a conservationist's nightmare but it has resulted in corridors of relatively undisturbed scrub-woodland, sustaining populations of the once-rare cowslip, providing a hunting ground for kestrels and even a habitat for orchids.

Motorways have also resulted in a spectacular spread of salt-marsh grass along verges and central reservations. This salt-tolerant coastal plant has spread inland to exploit the soils made salt rich by winter treatment of roads. Foreign plant invaders have also got a foothold. One interesting example is Oxford ragwort, so called because it was introduced to the botanical gardens of Oxford from its native habitat on the volcanic slopes of Mount Etna in Sicily in 1690. This plant is a vigorous coloniser and it managed to escape and establish itself on the walls of the city. There it remained until the coming of the railways in 1879. Now the distribution map of Oxford ragwort mirrors exactly the spread of the railways from the home counties to the rest of the country. Its success was due to the ash and cinder laid along rail tracks, providing soil characteristics just like its volcanic home.

Other invaders have been more of a nuisance. The sycamore tree, introduced to Britain from Mediterranean climes, has established itself as a vigorous competitor, often forcing out native oak and ash in mixed woodlands. Sycamore supports only 30 species of animals compared with the 150 or so that can live on oak, resulting in poorer diversity in woodland. In water, plants spread quickly and can soon clog up ponds, canals and lakes, speeding up succession to marsh. One recent pest is the pygmy weed from New Zealand, introduced on plants imported for garden ponds. The problem is made worse because the weed continues to grow right through the winter months and will sprout from any tiny piece that breaks off.

See CD-ROM:
Dunes and marsh and Swamps

Figure 7.7 Invading species which cause problems

See CD-ROM:
Habitats and Swamps

A pond badly weeded up by New Zealand pygmy weed (*Crassula helmsii*)

Water hyacinth can soon spread across whole lakes choking them

In Australia, an invasion of the prickly pear cactus threatened to wipe out huge areas of productive sheep pasture. A natural herbivore, the cinnabar moth, was introduced to control the pest. Imports from the Indian subcontinent include rhododendron, which has escaped into woodland and throttles plants of the shrub layer, and Himalayan balsam, whose waxy seeds spread quickly in water and infest river banks, forcing out native plants.

See CD-ROM:
Desert plants and Woodlands

Activities: Conservation and sustainability (KS2)

Visit a local nature reserve or invite members of a conservation group or people connected with a nature reserve to speak to children.

- Ask children to find out about what the reserve is trying to do and how it is managed. Get them to make a map of the reserve and to mark on things that have been done, e.g. planting of trees.

- Give children a map of an urban area or of the school grounds. Ask them to research from books what plants would be best to enhance the area and why they would choose these types, e.g. shelter from wind, food and homes for animals, interesting colours of leaves at different times of the year.
- If you have a school pond or wildlife area, get children to take photographs showing the change in the habitat over a year. Ask children to plan out management actions over the year and to organise how these will be carried out.
- Provide pictures of an urban (derelict) environment and ask children to think of ways it could be enhanced. Build a model to show the improvements.
- Collect examples of local planning proposals. Look for examples of green space. Are any tree plantings planned? What types will be planted? What size will gardens be?
- Go to a DIY centre and look at packaging. How much of the material is from sustainable forests?

Children's ideas about plants and the environment

- Children can think of few plant types in habitats compared with animals. Make sure you provide plenty of plant examples when you plan activities.
- Children tend to think of plants growing in pots and often draw these rather than plants surrounded by other plants and in natural surroundings.
- Children reason that one level of a food chain has been provided to feed the next. For example they might say: "There are more rabbits than foxes because the foxes have to have enough to eat", or: "Plants make food for the animals to eat".

In fact the reason that each level of a food chain has fewer individuals – or less mass – than the one preceding it is because only about a tenth of the energy can be transferred from one organism to another. See Figure 4.2, showing how much of the sun's energy ends up in a beefburger, on page 40.

Literacy links

Vocabulary

Key Stage 1	Key Stage 2
Beech	Adaptation
Birch	Canopy
Camouflage	Carnivore
Environment	Community
Field	Conservation
Habitat	Consumer
Hedge	Ecosystem
Meadow	Energy
Moor	Food chain
Oak	Food web
Woodland	Herbivore
	Producer
	Quadrat
	Sustainable

Literacy-related activities	Most suitable for NC year
Match plants and animals with their names and the places where they live.	R/Y1
Make question cards for a display connected with a particular habitat studied: What animals live and nest in the trees? What animals come out at night? How many animals eat the leaves of . . .?	Y2
Write a newspaper–style report entitled *'If you go down to the woods today'*, describing what it might be like to live in a beech, oak or birch woodland.	Y3/4
Compose questions to ask a wildlife expert on a visit to a reserve or for someone visiting school to talk to the class.	Y4
Write a letter to a nature warden or environmental officer to ask how a nature reserve is managed and what wardens have to do during the year.	Y4/5
Ask children to compose a set of arguments in support of tree planting, making a school pond or wild meadow.	Y5/6

Text-related work

Fiction and poetry
The Very Hungry Caterpillar can be used with young children to talk about the idea of food chains and how all animals depend in some way on plants (KS1).

The children's poem *The Intruder*, by James Reeves, links well with work on woodland habitats and camouflage. *The Dream of the Cabbage Patch Caterpillars* by Libby Houston deals with the different plant foods that caterpillars and butterflies exploit during their life cycle – see Chapter 11 page 144 (KS1 and KS2).

There are a number of stories that deal with environmental issues – see Chapter 11 for details (KS1 and KS2).

Non-fiction
Collect examples of DIY products that use plant materials and look for examples of labelling which mention use of sustainable resources (KS2).

Look at reports in papers dealing with environmental issues, e.g. conservation of habitats, building of a new park, etc. Discuss with children how these reports are structured and get children to write a report for the press on a scheme they would like to put forward (KS2).

Numeracy and information and communications technology (ICT) links

See CD-ROM:
Habitats, Tropical
and *Desert plants*

Activities related to numeracy objectives	Objectives relevant to NC year
Record findings from surveys of habitats using a tally system (see activities on page 86).	Y4
Record the cover of plants in a quadrat as fractions, e.g. 1/4, 1/2, 1/3, 3/4, 1/10, or as percentage of cover (see page 84).	Y4 Y5

ICT links	Relating to QCA unit
Photocopy leaf shapes and add labels to make an identification sheet for a field trip.	4B
Use a computer to make a chart of when plants around the school come into flower. Use the colouring options to fill in the chart to show the pattern – see the example in this chapter on page 87.	5B
Use environmental probes to measure the amount of light and moisture in a habitat.	
Use a CD-ROM, e.g. *Garden Wildlife* (see Chapter 11 page 145) to find out what animals and plants live in common urban habitats.	
Use images from the CD-ROM to make displays and information books about world habitats such as deserts and rainforests.	

Are plants the same in different places?

What plants can you find in these places? Draw and name plants you find.

Place	*I found . . .*
Wall	
Cracks in the playground	
Path across the school field	
Near a hedge	
In the middle of the school field	
In a flower bed	
On a lawn	

Surveying plants

Are there more daisies at the top or at the bottom of a slope?
Do more dandelions grow near to paths?
Which plants can stand trampling?

These questions can be answered by carrying out a plant survey. First you
will need a wooden or wire square, called a *quadrat*, and a tape measure.

● Lay your tape measure or a piece of string out across a slope or path or
somewhere else you want to study.

● Put your quadrat over the tape at 2 metre intervals. Record the plants
that are there using the six-point scale shown in the table below.

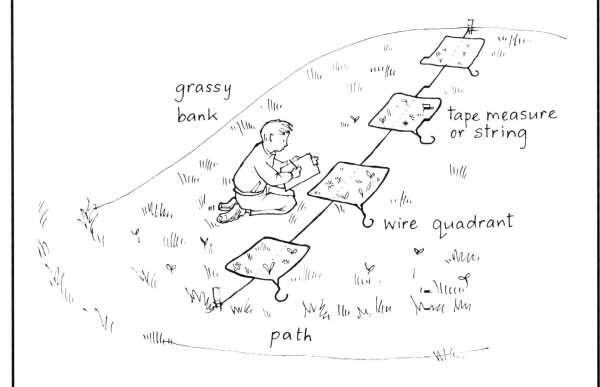

Copiable worksheet 7.2 *continued*

Fill in this results table as you carry out your survey.

Types of plants	Six–point scale of plant abundance						
	0	1	2	3	4	5	6
	No plants	Only one or two	A few plants	At least a quarter of the quadrat is covered	Plants are common in the quadrat	Plants are very common. More than half the quadrat is covered	Plants dominate the quadrat. Most of it is covered by them.
Clover							
Daisy							
Dandelion							
Moss							
Buttercup							
Speedwell							
Medick							
Cats-ear or thistle							

- What patterns can you see in your results?

- Is there more of a particular plant in one part of your line than another?

Copiable worksheet 7.2 *continued*

- Pick a type of plant that shows a pattern in its distribution and draw a bar chart to show the pattern.

- Write a title for your graph like the one shown below.

A bar graph to show the pattern of abundance

of _____ across _____

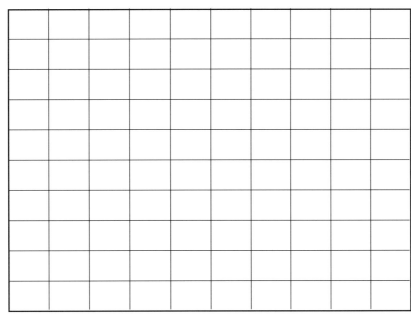

Abundance

Quadrats ⟶

- What might have caused more of this plant to be in one place than another?

- Design an investigation to find out if this was the cause.

Chapter 8

Mighty microbes

Microbes, or more properly *micro-organisms,* are not strictly plants, but without them the communities we looked at in Chapter 7 would not exist. Microbes come in all shapes and sizes, and stories associated with them are fascinating. The number of different types is vast. There are 1.5 million types of fungi alone, and this is probably just 5% of what could be out there. Microbes affect our lives in many ways, both good and bad.

National Curriculum links:
Key Stage 2: Sc1 1a; Sc2 5f

PSHE guidelines:
Key Stage 1: 3c Spread of diseases.
Key Stage 2: 3b Microbes and disease.

Links with units in the QCA scheme of work for science:
6B Micro-organisms.

What are microbes?

The programme of study in the National Curriculum for science defines them as 'living organisms that are often too small to be seen'. They come from a number of different groups of living things. Tiny, single-celled creatures called *protozoa* are animals and *algae* are plants. *Bacteria, viruses* and *fungi* are neither plant nor animal. Their bodies are not built in the same ways as most living things and they feed differently.

As far as size goes, there is huge variation.

Figure 8.1 Relative size of microbes

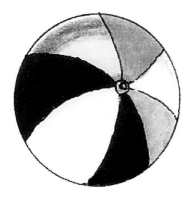 

Microbes vary in size. If each of the following were magnified 50,000 times then a fungus cell would be the size of a beach ball, an algal cell – a football, a bacterium – a golf ball, and a virus – the size of a full stop!

Fungi, including mushrooms, toadstools and moulds, are more likely to be studied by children, and these all produce obvious reproductive structures called fruiting bodies, much larger than anything in the pictures above.

See CD-ROM: *Fungi*

Microbes for good – nature's recyclers

In Chapter 4 we saw that the energy from the Sun trapped by plant producers is fed through different levels of animal life called consumers, with a loss of energy at each transfer. These levels of life and features of the environment, like soil, air, water and nutrients, make up what we call an *ecosystem*. There is one more vital living component, and without it the system would suffocate in its own waste and collapse. These are the *decomposers* – nature's recyclers. Many decomposers are microbes, mainly fungi and bacteria, which break down dead material in the process of decay and release vital nutrients like nitrogen, phosphorus and potassium that were locked up in the tissues of plants and animals.

Children can study the effect that nutrients have on plants by adding different amounts of fertiliser to growing seedlings. Fertilisers are now sold in convenient pellet form, and if you add these to plants with low variability (i.e. the changes that you see are not likely to be determined by its genetics), a worthwhile experiment can be set up by older children (see copiable worksheet 8.2).

Fungi are some of the most obvious and efficient decomposers. They lack the cell structure of plants and animals and feed using a network of narrow tubes called *hyphae,* entwining and pervading dead and decaying material and turning it into a nutritious soup that can be absorbed into these tubes. Most of this activity goes on unseen beneath the surface of litter or soil. When it comes to reproduction, fungi sprout often spectacular fruiting bodies that push into the air. A puffball fungus once produced a fruiting body over 1 metre across and was reported as an object from outer space. The stinkhorn is so-called because it smells of rotting meat, attracting flies that will transport its spores.

Figure 8.2 Examples of fungal fruiting bodies

Coprinus   Gomphidius

See CD-ROM: *Fungi* Like flowerless plants (see page 14), fungi produce spores rather than seeds, that drift in clouds of countless millions through the air. When spores alight on the warm, moist, sugary surface of fruit or bread, they germinate and the feeding hyphae complete the cycle of decomposition.

Microbes control the vitality of an ecosystem. In a woodland everything is recycled: logs, twigs, leaves, dead animals. The speed of return of nutrients is very much down to the efficiency at which decomposers work. In the warmth of the tropics this is fast, which is why rainforests are so productive. In the Arctic, the frozen soil and short summers mean that recycling and nutrient uptake are painfully slow. Tundra plants can take hundreds of years to grow to full size.

Intensive agriculture robs the ecosystem of plant material that would naturally be recycled, quickly depleting the soil of its minerals. The land must be allowed to recuperate or have its minerals replenished through addition of organic waste or chemicals. If this basic law of agro-ecology is ignored, the consequences can be catastrophic. This happened in the crop growing areas of America resulting in the 'badlands' landscape.

Figure 8.3 A 'badlands' landscape resulting from erosion of soil following crop failure

See CD-ROM:
Conservation and green issues

Activities (KS2)

Safety! Fungi, including moulds, produce vast numbers of spores that can induce allergic reactions. Never allow children to open containers containing mouldy foods – see *Be Safe* (ASE, 1990 pages 20 – 21) for notes on the handling and disposal of microbe material.

Put samples of fresh moist bread, apple, orange and cheese into a plastic sweet jar and secure the lid with tape.

- Get children to observe the food samples over ten days and record the changes and the number and colour of different moulds seen. Ask them which moulds appear first and which foods have most mould at the end.
- Ask children to design an investigation to see if the amount of

moisture affects the amount of mould that grows on bread. Children might come up with the idea of using similar-sized pieces of bread, one dried by toasting and the others having different amounts of water added to them. The pieces of bread should be sealed in separate jars or plastic bags (see safety note).

- Children could also investigate the effect of temperature on mould growth by keeping moist bread in different places and recording how much mould develops.

Cut dead tree leaves into equally sized samples and place into three bags with different mesh sizes – use an onion bag, an orange bag and a pair of tights.

- Ask children to predict what will happen to the leaves if we bury the bags in soil. Will the leaves disappear at the same speed in each bag?
- Get children to bury the bags at an equal depth in soil and recover them after three weeks. Empty the contents and record the amount – mass or leaf area – remaining.

This experiment works on the principle that larger decomposers such as worms and woodlice, as well as microbes, can enter the bags with larger holes, and so the rate of leaf decomposition will be faster. The rate of decomposition will also be affected by the temperature, moisture and type of soil.

Microbes for good: the world's original biotechnology

The world's first biotechnology, brewing, is down to a fungus – yeast. A bottle of beer was recovered from a 3,000-year-old tomb in Egypt. The yeast sediment from the bottle still contained live cells and these were used to recreate the brew in 1994 – 'Tutankhamun Light Ale'!

Yeast feeds on sugar, converting it to carbon dioxide and alcohol. This can happen without the aid of oxygen in a special kind of respiration called *fermentation*. Yeasts occur naturally as white growth on the skins of fruits. When grapes decompose, the yeast on the skin ferments the sugar in the fruit converting the juice to wine. To make beer, the sugar is extracted from germinated barley seed, producing malt. Hops are added for flavour and the resulting mash is heated and then cooled so that the added yeast isn't killed – nature does the rest. For cider, the juice squeezed from apples is fermented. The carbon dioxide produced from fermentation can be harnessed to make bread dough rise. If it is allowed to accumulate in fermented drinks, the result is fizzy – like champagne.

Today, the manipulation of yeast is a multi-billion pound industry. Extracts from fermentation are used to make nutritious spreads like Marmite. Yeast has even been grown on petroleum waste in a chemical plant, producing 20,000 tonnes of protein every year. Researchers are currently engineering yeast strains that can produce collagen protein for use in surgery and to remove fat stains from clothes.

Another productive little fungus, *Fusarium,* can produce high quality food rich in protein and fibre and low in fat. This material, called mycoprotein, is sold as Quorn®, a common substitute for meat in pies and burgers.

Bacteria are also in on the biotechnology act. Yoghurts are made from special cultures of bacteria that sour and thicken milk in a controlled way. Bacteria reproduce very rapidly and their genetic material (DNA) is organised in a relatively simply way. Genes from a number of living organisms have been identified that can manufacture certain chemicals. When these genes are spliced into bacterial DNA, and the bacteria are fast-bred in huge vats, the result is chemical manufacture on a vast and cheap scale. Many drugs and chemicals are now made in this way.

Activities: Biotechnology (KS1 and 2)

Collect some small 'soda-pop' bottles. Place different mixtures of yeast, sugar and water into each bottle and leave in a warm place. Observe the changes. (See copiable worksheet 8.1)

- Make some bread dough using yeast. Cut the dough into three equal portions. Put one bag on top of a warm radiator, one in the classroom and one in a cold place (KS1).
- Measure the height and size of the dough after 30 minutes.
- Now bake each sample of dough in an oven according to the recipe. When cooked, cool and then cut the loaves.
- Observe and comment on the appearance of the bread.

The amount and rate of carbon dioxide that the yeast produces will determine the internal structure of the bread. The process is called 'proving' the dough. If the temperature is too high, the carbon dioxide will accumulate and burst at the top of the dough, and this is what has happened when you see holes at the top of some loaves. Baking in an oven raises the temperature to a level that kills off the yeast and prevents the process continuing.

Safety! Ensure that all utensils and surfaces are cleaned with disinfectant and that children have washed their hands.

Making yoghurt (KS2)

- Sterilise a vacuum flask with boiling water and add some warm UHT milk.
- Add a couple of spoonfuls of natural yoghurt, stir, and then seal the flask. Leave for about eight hours or overnight.
- You could ask the children to test the pH with a paper strip of the mixture before and after making the yoghurt.
- Get children to taste their yoghurt and explain all the changes they observe. They could add flavours, colours and types of fruit to their yoghurts and design their own varieties.

Microbes for bad – the fight against disease

All the groups of microbes we have mentioned have a downside. When they feed parasitically they can become *pathogens*, invading the human body and causing disease.

Human skin provides a tough, dry and hostile barrier and is even armed with its own microbes that can fight off would-be intruders. Some recent research showed that well-scrubbed children might be less healthy than ones with dirtier skins. The way in for pathogens is through holes in this defence. Microbes can sneak in through the mouth and nose when we inhale moisture droplets, on food and in drink, through sweat pores, through cuts, scratches and insect bites, and through penetrative sex. The table in Figure 8.4 on page 107 shows some examples of common diseases, the microbe type responsible, and ways in which they can enter the body.

Once the pathogenic microbe is inside, damage is done directly to cells by tearing their walls apart and attacking their contents or by the secretion of chemicals that digest cells. Bacteria produce nasty chemical poisons called *toxins* and these can have spectacular effects. The tetanus bacterium releases a toxin that sends the body's muscles into paralysing spasms, often leading to asphyxiation – hence the name lockjaw. In Napoleonic times, before the age of modern medicines, the only treatment was to knock out the victim's teeth and ram a pipe down the throat to let them breathe. Not many patients survived!

There are two methods by which the body attacks pathogens, both provided by blood. One type of white blood cell attacks microbes directly, flowing around them and ingesting the invader in a process called *phagocytosis*. A different type of white blood cell produces a protein called an *antibody*, which is capable of identifying a specific pathogen and neutralising it. Each time a microbe invades, the immune system draws on its bank of antibodies and selects the specific one for

Figure 8.4 Some common diseases

Disease	Microbe type	How it gets in
Influenza	Virus	On inhaled moisture droplets
Polio	Virus	In drinking water
Tetanus	Bacterium	From soil and objects on the ground through cuts
Measles	Virus	Inhalation
Malaria	Protozoan (single-celled animal)	Injected with the saliva of a mosquito when it bites
Syphilis	Bacterium	During penetrative sex
HIV (Human immunodeficiency virus)	Virus	Exchange of blood or body fluids and during penetrative sex
Athlete's foot	Fungus	Spores from soil or water attach to cuts and abrasions on foot

the job. Each invasion stimulates production of more antibodies, and new types are 'memorised' in case they are needed in the future.

Today the process of *vaccination* can boost this defence mechanism. A weakened strain of the pathogen, or some substances extracted from it, are introduced to the blood stream and this stimulates antibody production. A booster injection increases the level of immunity significantly.

The word *vaccination* comes from the Latin *vacca*, meaning 'cow'. The process owes its discovery to the bravery and scientific ability of a doctor called Edward Jenner. It is worth telling his story here, not least because the programme of study for science now mentions him.

In the late 18th century, one in every three people died of the horrible and disfiguring disease smallpox. Jenner noticed that milkmaids who had contracted a similar disease from cows, called cowpox, never caught smallpox. On 14 May 1796, Jenner started his daring experiment. He extracted the pus from a scab on a milkmaid with cowpox and scratched some of this into the arm of an eight-year-old called James Phipps. A week later the boy caught cowpox and was ill for a day or two. Jenner decided to leave him for a while and then on 1 July infected him with smallpox pus. Fortunately for Jenner, his hunch that something causing one disease could prevent another paid off, and James Phipps survived.

What is remarkable is that no-one at this time knew that microbes were involved. This had to wait nearly 50 years until the pioneering work of another great scientist, Louis Pasteur. The jealousy, suspicions and ignorance of the times meant that Jenner, was publicly vilified.

We are still just as suspicious of new scientific discoveries – only today we cannot use the excuse of public ignorance. Or can we? Food for thought...

Children's ideas about microbes and decay

- Children tend to associate decay with disappearance or human intervention. They rarely think of microbes.

In a question asking what happens to an apple when it rots, children claimed material from it soaked into the ground, disappeared into the air or was taken away by someone.

- Children rarely associate microbes with return of useful substances to the soil, even if they appreciate their role in decay.

Literacy links

Vocabulary

Key Stage 1	Key Stage 2
Fungus	Bacteria
Germ	Decay
Mould	Decompose
Mushroom	Disease
Toadstool	Fertiliser
	Microbe
	Minerals
	Nutrient
	Recycle
	Virus

Literacy-related activities	Most suitable for NC year
Ask children to write out a set of rules for keeping food fresh. The rules should be linked to evidence gained from investigations.	Y3
Get children to set out a reasoned argument to explain why leaves buried in a bag with large holes 'disappear' (break down) faster than leaves in a bag with small holes. Their reasoning should be in line with size of micro-organisms that might be involved.	Y4/5
Write out a set of instructions for making yoghurt.	Y4/5
Imagine you are Edward Jenner. Write a story of how you cured James Phipps of cowpox and include why you were convinced your idea would work.	Y6

Text-related work

Fiction and poetry
Ted Hughes' poem *Leaves* is a superb example of a poem dealing with decay and recycling – see Chapter 11 for this and other poems (KS2).

The story of *Fungus the Bogeyman* by Raymond Briggs provides a number of points for discussion about the role of microbes in decay and recycling (KS2).

Non-fiction
Look at labelling on food packaging to see instructions for storage (KS2).

Look at leaflets persuading people to vaccinate their children or to have injections before travelling. Look at ways the leaflets give information. Discuss reasons why some parents might be worried about vaccination for their children. NOTE: this may be a sensitive issue for some children (KS2).

Children could design their own leaflet or poster about this (KS2).

Numeracy and information and communications technology (ICT) links

Activities related to numeracy objectives	Objectives relevant to NC year
Draw a circle of 10cm diameter to represent a fungus cell. Now look in books to find relative sizes of other microbes and draw circles with different diameters to show the relative sizes – add drawings of each type of microbe to the paper circles and make a display.	Y4/5
Enter figures into a spreadsheet (*see below**) or use a calculator to double a number over and over again to model the increase in a population of bacteria (assume one bacterium splits into two every 30 minutes). How many will there be in an hour, after six hours, 12 hours, 24 hours?	Y5/6
Draw a graph of the results of the calculation above. This should be a line graph – help children with scale. You may only be able to graph a few hours of growth.	Y6

ICT links	Relating to QCA unit
Enter figures for bacterial growth into a spreadsheet and add a formula that will automatically calculate the next entry for a time 30 minutes later as a doubling of the previous figure. Use the computer to generate a line graph showing the results.	6B
Use a computer to design a leaflet, e.g. using *Microsoft Publisher*, that gives information about vaccination, e.g. against tetanus. Include a design to show what might happen to you if you got lockjaw.	4D, 5C

Yeast balloons

Put some water into five 'soda-pop' bottles.

Add different things to each one as shown below. Shake the bottles to mix them up.

When you have finished put a different coloured balloon over the top of each bottle.

| 1 | 2 | 3 | 4 | 5 |

Put yeast and sugar in this one.
Keep it in a warm place.

Put yeast and sugar in this one.
Put it in a cold place.

Put only yeast in this one – NO SUGAR.
Keep it in a warm place.

Put yeast and sugar in this one.
Give it to your teacher to boil the mixture.

Put only sugar in this one – NO YEAST.
Keep it in a warm place.

Leave your experiment for about an hour and then record what you see in this table:

Balloon colour	What the bottle contained	What has happened?	What can you see inside the bottle?

- What happened to some of the balloons?

- Why did some balloons get bigger than others?

- Could it be the yeast that has done this or the sugar? How can you tell from your results?

- What might be made by the yeast that could make the balloons get bigger?

- Why didn't the yeast work when it had been boiled?

Let's make a super radish

Gardeners often hold competitions to see who can grow the biggest leek, onion, and so on. Some people say that they grow huge vegetables by giving their plants lots of fertiliser.

Will you be able to grow big radishes if you put lots of fertiliser in some growing pots with the seeds?

In this investigation you will find out how much fertiliser is needed to grow the biggest radish.

1. Take a black tub of the type 35mm film comes in, make a 2mm hole in its base and insert a wick into the hole.

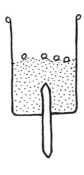

2. Take a 'growing mix' of equal parts peat and vermiculite and half fill the tub with it. Place four slow-release fertiliser pellets on top of this.

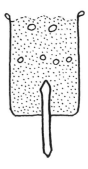

3. Fill almost to the top with growing mix. Place in two or three radish seeds and lightly cover with more growing mix.

4. Carefully add water until it drips from the wick. Place the tub on capillary matting standing on a reservoir of water, under a light-bank.

5. After four to five days, thin the growth to leave just one healthy seedling per tub.

6. After 16-20 days, the 'super radishes' will be ready for harvesting.

Copiable worksheet 8.2 *continued*

1. Change the amount of fertiliser you put in each film can, e.g. two, four, six, eight, ten fertiliser pellets. Some groups could set up experiments using more pellets and you could share results as a class.

2. Should you set up one can with no fertiliser pellets added?

3. Where should the plants be kept to make the tests fair? What else must you keep the same when you set up your cans?

4. When your plants are mature (16-20 days), you can harvest your radishes – but how will you tell which ones have been most successful? What will you measure? Think of at least two measurements you can make.

5. Make a table to show all your results.

6. Make a graph to show your results. Which type of graph should you use? You could use a computer to help you draw a graph.

7. Use your results to say if you think it is true that the more fertiliser, the bigger the radish. What is the best amount of fertiliser to use?

Chapter 9

Celebrating with plants

Aт six in the morning on the second Friday in August every year, a man enters the town hall in Queensferry, Edinburgh and has the sticky fruits of burdock plastered all over his body – special care is needed for the sensitive areas. It takes three hours to complete his costume. Garlands of flowers are woven for his head-dress and then he must stagger through the streets carrying two heavy wooden poles festooned with flowers. This is the 'Burry Man'. His costume is a kind of communal hair shirt, worn to absolve the sins of his town. Traditions like this were once commonplace in Britain and, though many are still alive, few people today appreciate how deeply connected we are with plant folklore.

Plants are powerful images but the origins of these are often obscure. All four countries of the British Isles have flowers as emblems. The greenery of Christmas has pagan origins in the celebration of woodland spirits and fertility rites. Even modern 'pop culture' uses plant symbolism. The film *American Beauty* used red roses to represent order, love, beauty, rebirth and, finally, death and enlightenment.

Figure 9.1 Children 'beating the bounds' – an ancient tradition on Ascension Day

National Curriculum links: There are a number of possible links with the National Curriculum for science and other subjects but there are equally important links to guidelines in the following areas:

Learning across the curriculum: See Pupils' cultural development – Key Stages 1 & 2.

PSHE guidelines: See Key Stage 2 Developing good relationships and respecting differences between people 4a, b, c, f.

See CD-ROM: *Celebrations*

In Chapter 7 on plants and the environment, I said that Britain was once covered in deciduous woodland. It is no surprise, therefore, that our ancestors held woods and their trees in awe, often conferring magical and medicinal properties on them. The oak had special significance. The Druids worshipped individual specimens and believed that anything driven into them would cause toothache. Young men carried acorns to preserve their youth, and milkmaids tied oak twigs to their buckets to stop the milk turning sour.

See CD-ROM:
Ancient plants

Many of our churches are surrounded by ancient yew trees. Some sites were pagan groves, and in medieval times yews were planted to ward off witches and next to graves as a sign of everlasting life.

Trees are also important in non-European cultures. In Korea, food is placed onto piles of stones under trees as it is believed they take up the spirits of the dead. In China, trees are planted on graves to prevent corruption of the body and to strengthen the soul. Evergreen cypress and pine are considered best for this as they do not lose their leaves in winter and therefore have more vitality.

Perhaps today, in the consumer-dominated world of online shopping and fast foods, it is time to re-establish some of the ancient traditions of plant lore. Children grow up in an increasingly multicultural society where old traditions are intermingled with ones from other countries. How often do we take time in school to find out about these other traditions and how they are celebrated? It is just as important to recognise the diversity of cultural tradition in an all-white school as it is in one that has children from different ethnic backgrounds. This helps all children to respect non-English traditions and dispels the ignorance on which racism can feed in later life.

See CD-ROM:
Celebrations

In this chapter we look at a number of examples of festivals and traditions that can be celebrated throughout the school year. I have concentrated on the plants of these festivals, but it is important to remember that there are many other features that can be used to stimulate work in school. There are inevitably some festivals missing, but there are excellent resources that you can consult for a more complete picture, e.g. *The Shap Calendar* and various websites – see Chapter 11 page 148). I have included a number of British non-religious and traditional celebrations, for example the four saints' days, because it is also important to remember the cultural diversity in the UK and Ireland.

The activities suggested are not just science-based. There are opportunities here for some excellent cross-curricular work that could support teaching in the new area of PSHE and citizenship, as well as more traditional areas such as art, music, technology and, of course, the Literacy Hour. Remember, too, that this type of work is an excellent way of linking school with the community. Most schools can find parents and friends who have knowledge of other cultures to come in and help out.

Time of year	Festival or celebration	Religion/culture	Main traditions	Special plants and foods	Suggestions for activities
January or February	Chinese New Year; Yuan Tan	Partly Buddhist	Celebrates the start of the first lunar month; gold and red are themes seen in dance, costume and decorations; gifts, sweets and money are given.	The kumquat plant is often seen in Chinese homes – its golden fruits are available in supermarkets as *physalis* or lantern fruits.	• Give children some *physalis* to taste. • Decorate red envelopes with gold paint or paper and put pressed flowers inside. • Prepare a Chinese feast and hold a class tasting session. • Let children see natural plant ingredients like ginger root, bean sprouts and water chestnuts.
1 March	St David's Day	Christian; Welsh national day	The feast of St David – son of the Prince of Cardiganshire who became a priest and died in AD 544.	Leek and, of course, the daffodil.	• Make leek and potato soup, Welsh cakes and *cawl* (lamb stew with parsley). • Look at the structure of leeks and daffodils. • Draw and name parts of the daffodil flower. • Look at bulbs and other methods of propagation (see Chapter 6).
Early March	Holi	Hindu	Holi welcomes the coming of spring. The holiday celebrates the defeat of Holika, who raided villages eating children. Holika was destroyed by burning torches thrown by the villagers. There are bonfires and people throw red, pink and yellow powdered dye and water over each other.	The coloured dyes were extracted from the Holi flower and squirted using water pistols made of bamboo. On the eve of the festival the Holi tree is burned. The Holi feast includes *daho wada*, made from raw jackfruit, and *malpua*, made from maida, milk, sugar and dried fruits.	• Extract dye from plant materials and spices such as turmeric. Use these to make tie-dyed scarves or T-shirts. • Make and taste *malpua*. • Investigate a number of dried fruits and compare them to see how much water they absorb. • Read some of the legends of Holi to children.

Time of year	Festival or celebration	Religion/culture	Main traditions	Special plants and foods	Suggestions for activities
17 March	St Patrick's Day	Christian; Irish national day	Feast day of the patron saint of Ireland. Celebrated by Irish communities across the globe – especially in the USA. St Patrick used the three leaves of the shamrock to illustrate the divine trinity.	Sprigs of shamrock a type of small white-flowered clover, are worn. Green is the theme.	• Look for examples of clover amongst grass. • Cook and taste *barm brach*, Irish teacake and potato cakes. • Plant out seed potatoes in the garden or in pots. • Read stories about the Irish potato famine. See CD-ROM: *Celebrations*
Third Sunday in March	Mothering Sunday	Traditional/modern	The Sunday halfway through Lent when young people living away from home were given time off work to visit their mothers. On the journey a bunch of wildflowers was picked as a present.	Bouquets of flowers, potted flowering plants and bulbs.	• Prepare a bunch of flowers picked from the garden – consider issues of which ones to choose, how many to pick, etc. • Plant bulbs in pots to flower for Mothering Sunday. • Design and make cards on a floral theme. See CD-ROM: *Celebrations*
March or April	Palm Sunday and Easter	Christian	Marks the first day of Holy Week and the triumphal entry of Jesus into Jerusalem. Palm leaves were placed before him. Easter was the time of pagan rites of rebirth. The Norse goddess of Spring was *Eostre* – hence the name, Easter.	Palm leaves are woven as a cross. Palm branches are often placed above houses until after Easter in southern Europe. Pace eggs in northern England are decorated with plant symbols of corn and clover signifying peace and rebirth. See CD-ROM: *Celebrations*	• Look at the shape of palm leaves and similar house plants. • Children act out the story of Jesus' entry to Jerusalem with palm leaves made from paper and card. • Children taste hot cross buns. • Make pace eggs (blown or hard boiled eggs) dyed with vegetable colour and painted with floral and corn designs.

Time of year	Festival or celebration	Religion/culture	Main traditions	Special plants and foods	Suggestions for activities
Early April	Hanamatsuri	Japanese Buddhist	A festival marking Buddha Shakyamuni's birthday in a garden in 565 BC.	Many floral shrines are created in the house and garden.	• Look at how plants/flowers are used in different cultures to mark birth, marriage and death.
13/14 April	Baisakhi	Sikh	Celebration of the founding of the Khalsa holy order by the Guru Gobind Singh in 1699. Harvest celebrations also occur and may be associated with a *mela* or fair.	In the Punjab (main Sikh state of India) the harvest celebrations last three days. In Britain one of the largest annual *melas* is in Bradford: a huge craft, arts, music and food fair.	• Children could explore a variety of Punjabi traditional foods and spices. • Children design and create their own *mela* in school celebrating arts, crafts, clothes and foods from a number of cultures.
April	Passover	Judaism	Eight-day festival commemorating the exodus of the Jews from slavery in Egypt. The *seder* meal is held at the start of the festival and has a menu of traditional foods, most with religious and historical significance.	*Matzah* (unleavened bread) made without yeast is eaten; Bitter herbs are a reminder of the hard life in exile in the desert. Coconut pyramids signify those that slaves helped construct.	• Read or enact the story of the Jews' from slavery to the promised land. • Connect events in the story to Jewish festivals across the year. • Look at the menu for a *seder* meal and connect all the items with religious and historic meaning.
21 April or 40th day after Easter	Ascension day or Holy Thursday	Christian	Last earthly appearance of the risen Christ who ascended into heaven on this day. Used to be customary for children to 'walk the bounds' of their parish and to be brushed with sticks as they did, in a tradition known as the 'beating of the bounds'.	Sticks of willow were used to 'beat the bounds'.	• Look at ancient and recent maps of your parish and chart the changes. • Beat the bounds around the school grounds. • Celebrate areas of change and development in and around the school, e.g. the planting of new trees, the renovation of a park, etc.

See CD-ROM: *Celebrations*

Time of year	Festival or celebration	Religion/culture	Main traditions	Special plants and foods	Suggestions for activities
23 April	St George's Day	Christian; English national day	St George lived and died in Palestine in the 4th Century and was first used as a national figure by Crusaders 1,000 years later. The popularity of parades grew in Victorian times. Red and white theme of the flag of England.	The red rose.	• Enact or tell the legend of St George and the dragon. • Make and bake bread buns proved with yeast. Serve with a variety of English cheeses. • Children could look at how the emblem of the rose is used in England and its history, e.g. red rose of Lancaster, white rose of Yorkshire. • Research the origins of rose-hip syrup used to feed children in the second World War.
1 May	May Day	English Traditional	Superimposed on an ancient Celtic festival called *Beltane* celebrating the beginning of summer. Dancing round the maypole, the crowning of the May Queen and morris dancing may all be derived from ancient fertility rites.	Young people gathered greenery and flowers and decorated their homes to signify the fertility of nature. Birch boughs decked with red and white rags were propped up against barns to protect horses against witches. A leaf-clad Jack-in-the-green featured in ancient May Day parades.	• Practise and perform maypole and morris dances. • Collect greenery and flowers and design and make wreaths to decorate the classroom. • Make imitation wreaths from coloured tissue paper entwined with plastic imitation greenery and wire. • Design a Jack-in-the-green costume and hold a May Day parade around the school or in an assembly.
September	Rosh Hashana	Judaism	The Jewish New Year celebrating the creation. The blowing of a ramshorn in the synagogue signifies Abraham's sacrifice of a ram in place of his son.	Apples dipped in honey are eaten in the hope of a sweet year.	• Children could make and taste toffee apples and prepare other recipes combining fruits with honey and other sweet foods. • Look for examples of other celebrations that include sweets, e.g. Guy Fawkes night.

Time of year	Festival or celebration	Religion/culture	Main traditions	Special plants and foods	Suggestions for activities
29 September	Michaelmas	Traditional/northern European	Traditionally the feast of St Michael who is said to have driven Satan from heaven. The harvest spirit was believed to have been driven into the last remaining swathes of corn.	Folklore has it that blackberries were unfit to eat until after this date as the devil spat on them when he was expelled from heaven. Corn stalks were woven into a corn dolly, which sat at the harvest supper. It was kept in the house until spring when it was ploughed into the land to work its magic on the new crop.	• Children could make collections of autumn fruits and study the ways in which these are used to disperse seeds (see Chapter 6). • Try using fruits like blackberries and elderberries to make dyes and decorate clothes with autumn leaf and fruit designs. • Look at designs for corn dollies – make them and display until spring – dig them into the school garden in spring.
September/ October	Harvest Festival	Traditional/northern European/British	A more recent and common tradition celebrated by most churches since the mid 19th century. Specially written hymns are sung and the church is decorated with displays of fruits and vegetables as well as flowers. More recently it has become a tradition to distribute produce to the needy.	Many different examples of farm and garden produce are displayed. Wild fruits and berries may also be included to signify nature's bounty. Real corn sheaves and bread baked in the shape of sheaves and corn dollies (see above) are also common.	• Children could collect and bring produce to school for a harvest festival. • Children and their teachers should choose a group or charity to donate produce to. It is best to involve all children in some way. • Decorate the school hall or classroom for a class or school harvest festival – practise and sing harvest hymns.

Time of year	Festival or celebration	Religion/culture	Main traditions	Special plants and foods	Suggestions for activities
September/ October	Sukkot – the feast of the tabernacles	Judaism	Remembers the time when the Israelites wandered in the wilderness for 40 years before reaching the promised land. They lived in booths or *sukkot* made from the branches and leaves of whatever plants they could find.	*Sukkot* are made in people's gardens and yards or in the synagogue. They must include the four traditional plants: *Lulav* – palm; *etrog* – citrus fruit; *hadas* – myrtle and *aravah* – willow. Incense and orange are fragrances associated with this festival. Paper flowers are common decorations in the house.	● Children could make a *sukkot* in one corner of the classroom. It should include a number of citrus fruits hung from inside. ● Ask a local rabbi to come to school to talk to children about the traditions of Judaism and the special prayers said at Sukkot. ● Look at other forms of temporary shelter made by nomadic peoples from plants.
				See CD-ROM: *Celebrations*	*See CD-ROM:* *Celebrations*
October/ November	Divali, Diwali or Deppavali – the festival of lights	Hindu (Sikh)	Held on the darkest night of the lunar month. This is the festival of lights and has various interpretations in different regions. Fireworks are common. Lakshmi, the goddess of wealth and prosperity, may be worshipped. At this time Sikhs celebrate the release of the sixth Guru, Guru Hargobind Singh, from Gwalior prison. It is a time for new clothes and the giving of sweets.	Few direct associations with plants but included here because it is one of the most important festivals of the year for the Asian communities in the UK.	● Schools can do useful work on light, colour and candle/lamp design to link with this festival. Susan Humphries has many useful suggestions in her book *Working Together* (see Chapter 11 page 137).

Time of year	Festival or celebration	Religion/culture	Main traditions	Special plants and foods	Suggestions for activities
30 November	St Andrew's Day	Christian; Scottish national day	St Andrew is the patron saint of Scotland and Russia. He was supposedly the brother of Peter and a fisherman on Lake Galilee. Tradition has it that he was crucified on an X-shaped cross in Achaia in northern Greece and his remains brought to Scotland – hence the shape of the St Andrew's cross of Scotland, part of the Union Jack.	The Scottish emblem is the thistle, possibly borrowed from the French by the Stewart kings in the 15th century. It stood for prickly aggression against invaders (the English – see the film *Braveheart*). 'Neeps and tatties' and oatcakes are traditional Scottish dishes eaten on this day.	● Get children to collect various examples of tartan and link them with different Scottish clans. ● Make 'neeps and tatties' from boiled and mashed potatoes and turnips seasoned with pepper. ● Make and taste traditional Scottish oatcakes and porridge. ● Children could also collect and paint thistles and look for other examples of flowers associated with different countries.
25 December	Christmas	Christian	Celebrating the birth of Jesus Christ but absorbing many traditional pagan rituals of the sun's rebirth following the winter solstice on 21 December. The Roman festival of Saturnalia occurred around this time. This has always been a significant time of feasting and celebration across northern Europe, when food and drink were taken in large measures to ease the pain of the dark, cold months – so not much has changed!	Burning of the yule log: Yule is associated with the Norse god Ullr. The Christmas tree and evergreen plants including holly and ivy were believed to shelter woodland spirits. The idea of having a conifer as decoration in the house is a German tradition supposedly introduced by Prince Albert, Queen Victoria's German husband. Mistletoe was believed by Druids to be the seminal fluid of the oak tree and therefore a sign of fertility – hence the tradition of kissing under it.	● Children could look at the issue of sustainability and recycling in relation to growth and replanting of Christmas trees. ● Collect examples of cards depicting plants used at Christmas – they could compare Victorian and modern designs. ● Learn the difference between evergreen and deciduous trees and show children the wide variety of species now used at Christmas. ● Look at mistletoe and find out where and how it grows – it is a parasite, e.g. growing on oak and apple trees. ● Sing the carol *The Holly and the Ivy*. Talk about the religious connections in the words. See CD-ROM: *Celebrations*

Time of year	Festival or celebration	Religion/culture	Main traditions	Special plants and foods	Suggestions for activities
Date progresses: Early November 2002	Ramadan	Islam	The Muslim year follows the pre-Gregorian, Arabic lunar calendar and so the festival moves forward by ten or eleven days each year. Muslims fast and pray between sunrise and sunset for one month. Fasting is one of the five pillars of the Islamic faith. Children may be encouraged to fast but it is not compulsory. Readings from the holy book, the Qu'ran, take place in the mosque each day.	The daily fast is traditionally broken by eating dates and drinking water.	● There are few direct activities here – see below for Eid.
Date progresses: Early December 2002	Eid-ul-Fitr	Islam	This festival signifies the end of Ramadan with the appearance of the new moon. This is a time for family reunions, feasts, the giving of presents and the wearing of new clothes. Gold and red are traditional colours of clothes, greeting cards and decorations.	Various sweet dishes served including sweet rice and *jelaybies* – deep-fried sweet rice and date cakes; Traditionally the Eid feast is set out on a cloth or blanket spread out in the desert. The dishes are presented *meze* style and these often include vegetables.	● Prepare a *meze* feast with the help of recipes and advice from a member of the Islamic community. ● Hold the feast outside if the time of year is right. ● Get children to make happy Eid cards decorated in Islamic designs, e.g. gold on blue. ● Learn Happy Eid in Urdu and put this on cards. ● Learn about dates and other fruits grown in the Middle East – hold a tasting session.

Chapter 10

Progressive plants

THIS PENULTIMATE chapter is not about flower power in the 1960s as the title might suggest! We are concerned here with how to provide experiences that challenge children and allow them to develop their scientific ideas. The education world calls this *progression*, which is a key feature of the National Curriculum for science.

Merely providing work in line with the requirements of the programmes of study in the National Curriculum documents will not ensure progression. The publication of a scheme of work for science by the Qualifications and Curriculum Authority (QCA, 2000) has gone some way to addressing the issue in terms of content, but Ofsted still criticise the lack of progression and differentiation, particularly in practical science (science attainment target 1 – scientific enquiry). Since scientific enquiry (Sc1) is weighted so highly in primary science assessment (50% at Key Stage 1 and 40% in Key Stage 2) and enquiry is a foundation for content learning, it is important to understand how progression works in this area.

In this chapter I show what progression means for the teacher and child learning and doing science. I also provide some examples of how investigations using plants can be made progressive in terms of the design of a task and what you might expect children to do – the learning outcomes. This features as a series of 'flowerpots', each relating to a level of National Curriculum attainment. A way you can support children in their planning of investigations – using a 'planning flower' is also included. This can be copied for use by children (see copiable worksheet 10.1).

How children progress in scientific enquiry (Sc1)

There are three main routes through which children develop and progress as they do practical work in science:

- the ways in which they tackle questions and challenges;
- the ways in which they learn to use the 'process skills' of scientific enquiry;
- the ways in which they use and draw on their scientific ideas.

Progression in challenging questions

As children learn to tackle questions and challenges they will become increasingly confident at how to deal with the question and to turn it into a form that can be investigated. They will also depend less on the help of their teacher in deciding what to do, how to record and display findings and what these might mean. Children will also handle equipment with increasing dexterity and develop an understanding of safety and ethical or environmental issues when designing enquiries.

Progression in using process skills

A skill in science describes something specific that you can do, for example reading temperature on a thermometer, or using a hand lens in a way that gives the best view. A *process skill* implies something larger. Process skills define the main areas in which children work in practical science and the decisions they have to take. As children develop and progress in their use of process skills, they will:

- *observe* with more care and in more detail;
- *measure* with an increasing degree of accuracy – learning to take decisions on the best instrument for the job in hand;
- make *predictions* that increasingly explain why something might happen and what science their prediction is based on;
- *communicate* findings by designing their own *recording* methods and choosing which type of graph is most appropriate to display results and look for patterns;
- *interpret* and *explain* their findings by looking carefully at results, moving from simple connections between cause and effect to a deeper understanding of relationships between one factor and another;
- *reflect* on their findings and increasingly look at how reliable their results are in relation to their plans and the methods used for investigations and whether their conclusions can really be justified. The National Curriculum programmes of study refer to this as *evaluation*.

A more detailed view on how these process skills progress over Key Stages 1 and 2, and how teachers can help to develop them, can be found in the excellent guide *Developing Science in The Primary Classroom* by Wynne Harlen and Sheila Jelly (1997). This and other helpful books on practical science in primary schools can be found in Chapter 11 page 139 and 140.

Progression in scientific ideas

It is important to remember that children do practical work not just to learn how to do investigations, but also to learn about science and the world around them. As children develop investigative skills they should be able to link their practical work to their developing knowledge of science. For example, a child's investigation of the amount of light a plant needs for growth might be informed by their understanding of how plants get food using the Sun's energy. Knowledge and understanding of the science will help children to make informed predictions and hypotheses. Examples of these can be seen in the 'flowerpot models' below.

The outcomes of scientific enquiries may also lead to new understanding of science. A child might investigate plants grown in different colours of light and find that ones grown in green light don't do well. This discovery might make the child realise that a green plant reflects green light and that, if this is the only colour of light it gets, then it cannot make much food.

The 'flowerpot model' of progression

Each of the headed sections on pages 128-133 shows an investigation on plant growth. There are five of these, each referenced to an attainment level of the National Curriculum for science. Each 'flowerpot' shows a typical question that could be posed at each level (progression in question demand or challenge) and some expected outcomes from children linked to the three strands of the National Curriculum programme of study for scientific enquiry (Sc1):

- planning;
- obtaining and presenting evidence;
- considering evidence and evaluating.

These flowerpot models have been used very successfully in teacher training courses (see the example quoted by Roy Phipps – Chapter 11, page 140) and the idea can be used to differentiate and plan for scientific investigations in any topic area, e.g. forces, light, materials, etc.

Science coordinators may find this model particularly useful.

Level 1

How does a plant grow?

Planning
- With the help of an adult, the children suggest ideas about planting and growing seeds.

Obtaining and presenting evidence
- Children plant seeds and observe their germination and growth.
- They talk about what they see.
- They make a picture record, e.g. showing growth at the start, the middle and the end.

Considering evidence and evaluating
- Children can describe how the plant grows bigger or gets new leaves.

Level 2

What do plants need to grow?

Planning
- Following a whole-class introduction, children make some suggestions by asking questions such as: Do plants need . . . soil, water, light, warmth, food?
- The teacher gives pairs or groups of children one of these aspects to test.
- The children say/predict what they think will happen.
- The teacher helps children plant their seeds in conditions chosen during class discussion.
- The teacher encourages children and helps them to suggest where plant pots might be placed, how much soil to use, etc, so that tests are kept the same or controlled.

Obtaining and presenting evidence

- Children keep a diary showing changes.
- Children measure growth using non-standard measures such as unifix cubes.
- Children record their observations and measurements in a chart or table provided and labelled by the teacher.
- The teacher might help children to record their results using a pictograph, e.g. using a computer.

Considering evidence and evaluating

- Children can describe what has happened using words such as stem, leaf and seed.
- Children compare what they have found with what they thought would happen.

Level 3

Where do plants grow best?

Planning

- During whole-class discussion the teacher helps children to come up with some suggestions for what we might mean by *best*.
- One group predicts that plants will grow taller in warmer places.
- Children plan out a test of this prediction and the teacher challenges them to make it fair.
- The teacher helps children plan by using a planning flower – see copiable worksheet 10.1.

Obtaining and presenting evidence

- Children grow plants in warm and cold places and they give each plant the same amount of water and compost.

- They record the heights of their plants in centimetres and enter results in a table that the teacher has helped them design. They also make drawings of their plants and relate these to measurements.

Considering evidence and evaluating

- Children look at their results and say whether the pattern confirms their prediction or not.
- Children can make the link between the results and the question being investigated, e.g. Yes, I think the cold does make plants grow less.
- Children realise that the plants put in a warm place were a long way from the window and could have had less light. They suggest that next time they would have to make sure that the plants all get the same light or they won't know if it's the cold that stops the plants growing.

Level 4

How does soil type affect how plants grow?

Planning

- Children in groups list a number of factors that affect how a plant grows. They share these in class discussion.
- The teacher helps them to turn one of their ideas into a question that can be investigated.
- The children come up with an idea to grow the same type of seedlings in sand, compost and garden soil.
- They also realise that they must use the same amount of soil each time, the same sized container, and place all the pots in a light and warm place.
- They predict that garden soil will be best because it is *more natural.*

- They record their plans using a planning flower.

Obtaining and presenting evidence

- Children are given a template for a table but decide themselves what they will record and enter the columns and rows accordingly.
- They measure their seedlings each day in centimetres and also record some observations in words, e.g. colour and numbers of leaves.
- Children are given squared paper and record their findings in a bar chart – they have already been shown how to do this (see Chapter 2 page 21).

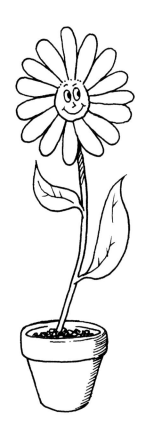

Considering evidence and evaluating

- Children look at their results and are able to see a pattern.
- They realise that plants grown in soil did not grow as high as those in compost and that those in sand only grew half as high as ones grown in soil.
- Children use information on the compost bag and find that compost is designed to provide good conditions for growth.
- Children reach conclusions using science ideas such as the fact that compost has a good balance and structure, and that it might contain food that plants need for growth. They realise that these features might not apply to all soils and suggest that not all soils are good for growth.
- Children realise that each pot may have contained different amounts of water at the start, even though they added equal amounts of water, and that this might have affected their results.

Level 5

How does fertiliser affect the growth of plants?

(See Chapter 8 page 102 for details on how to set up this investigation, and copiable worksheet 8.2.)

Planning

- Children suggest that plants will grow better the more fertiliser you add because fertiliser provides the nutrients or minor foods that plants need to grow well.
- They decide to add different amounts of a fertiliser (they do this by adding osmoscote pellets to plant pots using 0, 4, 8, 12, 16 pellets) to plants grown in similar containers. They use the same amount of compost in each pot and place them all under a light bank (see Chapter 3).
- The investigation is planned using planning sheets or planning boards.
- They design a table to record their results. They decide to record the height of their plants and the number of leaves after three weeks of growth.
- Children predict that the plants with 16 pellets will grow the most because they have the most nutrients and that will produce more leaves or growth.

Obtaining and presenting evidence

- The results are recorded in a table and the average number of leaves for each value of fertiliser is worked out.
- Children think about what graph to use to display results and they choose a line graph because they realise that they are graphing a change in amount (of fertiliser) against another change in amount (height of plants).

Considering evidence and evaluating

- Children look at their graphs and notice a pattern – that each addition of fertiliser causes more growth, but only up to a certain point, and that the plants with the most fertiliser did not grow to be the highest.
- Children also comment that the plants did not have very different numbers of leaves as they predicted, but that the plants with more fertiliser seemed to have bigger leaves. They suggest that measuring leaf area would have been a better idea than just counting leaves.
- Children put their findings and information from books together to suggest that plants with too much fertiliser might suffer. They find a phrase in a gardening book that refers to 'burning off' to explain this phenomenon.
- Children go on to design a poster to warn of the dangers of 'burning off' and refer to not wasting money and caring for the environment by not using so much of a chemical.

Supporting children's planning of investigations

Children can easily get lost in the planning process – losing sight of what it is that they are changing, measuring and keeping the same. A framework to help children keep track of what they are doing and trying to find out is, therefore, a good idea.

The one provided here is a 'planning flower' – after all this is a book about plants! Each petal represents a different aspect of an investigation. The planning moves clockwise around the flower, starting with the question that children are investigating and ending with a simple statement of what children have found out or examples of new learning.

At the lowest levels in progression (levels 1-3) the teacher will help children to enter the question to be investigated. By the time children have become more confident and practised planners, they can move away from the 'planning flower', but you might still want to remind them of these headings on a worksheet or the board.

The planning flower

Reproduced by permission of Ginn and Co. (1998), a division of Reed Elsevier.

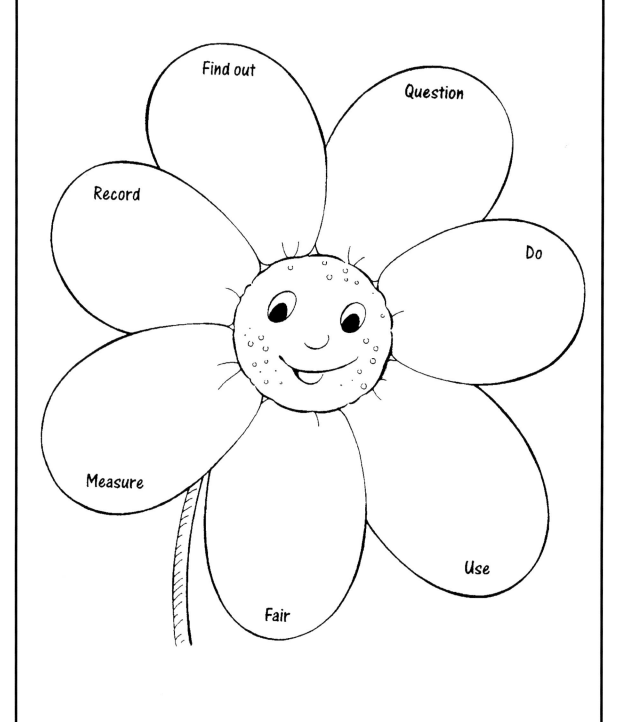

Chapter 11

Resources

THERE ARE many useful resources now available to help you teach good plant science at both primary key stages. Examples are listed in four sections:

1. Books, information and activity packs for the teacher.
2. Non-fiction books, stories and poetry for children to read and that support links with the Literacy Hour.
3. Information and communications technology resources including useful websites.
4. Organisations supporting plant science for schools, and places to visit.

There are notes about resources suggesting how you might use them.

1. Books, information and activity packs for the teacher

(A) Useful books and packs about plants providing background and ideas for the teacher

Source	Notes
Green Planet: The Story of Plant Life on Earth. ed. David M. Moore (1982). Cambridge University Press.	A wonderful, readable background book for the teacher – superbly produced – worth getting hold of a copy from a local library.
Woodlands: A Nature Guide. J.L. Cloudsley Thompson. Crowood Press.	Worth looking out for as a remaindered item in book sales or in libraries – a wonderful little book and very readable.
Star Science: Teachers Guides and Pupil's Books for 'The Environment' and 'Plant Life'. R. Feasey, R. Gott, R.Phipps, and J. Stringer, (1998). Ginn and Company.	These books from the popular primary science scheme have several useful activities and ideas for teachers to use. Includes the skills ladder, planning flower and the planning house to support investigations.
Plants for People. Anna Lewington (1990). Natural History Museum Publications.	One of the best books about plants and how they are used – a mine of fascinating information.
Flora Brittanica. Richard Mabey (1997). Chatto and Windus.	Simply a masterpiece. One of the best popular botanical books ever published. This book tells you about every British plant, its history and traditions.
Plants Across the Curriculum. Teacher's pack (1995). Royal Botanic Gardens, Kew.	Photographic, poster and video materials to support a visit to Kew but can also be used at Key Stage 2 to link plant work with art, English, geography, etc.
Trees in the School Grounds Rosemary Clark and Peter Walters (1992). Learning through Landscapes. Southgate Publishers.	Very good ideas for the teacher either around the school or when visiting parks, gardens and nature reserves.

Source	Notes
The Private Life of Plants. David Attenborough (1995). BBC Books.	The book based on a superb TV series broadcast in 1995. Contains lots of very interesting anecdotal information that children will find fascinating.
Festivals in World Religions. Brown, Alan ed. (1998). Longmans.	This book is produced by the Shap Working Party (see section on organisations) and gives details of many festivals and advice on teaching about world religions and other cultures.
Folklore, Myths and Legends of Britain. Readers' Digest (1973). London. The Reader's Digest Association Limited.	If this book is still in print it is worth getting for your own personal interest.
Working Together: Co-operative Learning Projects Involving the Whole School Community. Susan Humphries and Susan Rowe (1996). Forbes Publications.	Susan Humphries, Headteacher at the Coombes School in Berkshire, has shown all of us how important it is to involve the whole community in the life of the school. This book is essential for the staff library – many good ideas.
Action for Plants. Tate and Lyle Sugars (1998). BMA communications. The pack can be obtained from: Tate and Lyle Information Service, Althrop Studios, 4-6 Althrop Road, London SW17 7ED.	A very useful pack of ideas and activities. Contains an excellent set of cards with details and drawings of common plants – ideal for identification.

(B) Useful guides on science, investigations and linking science with literacy and numeracy

Source	Notes
Developing Science in the Primary Classroom. Wynne Harlen and Sheila Jelly (1997). Longmans.	One of the most useful guides to primary science that you can buy. Gives excellent guidance on progression steps in practical work and how these can be assessed and supported by the teacher.

Source	Notes
Making Sense of Primary Science Investigations. Anne Goldsworthy and Rosemary Feasey (1997). Association for Science Education.	Very good advice on planning, structuring and differentiating investigations – gives examples of how process skills such as graphing and designing tables progress across Key Stages 1 and 2.
'The Flowerpot Model'. Roy Phipps (1997), in *Questions of Maths and Science,* January issue pages 35-38	This article discusses progression and shows how the 'flowerpot model' shown in Chapter 10 can be used as an Inset activity.
Be Safe. Second Edition. The Association for Science Education (ASE). (1990). Pages 22-23.	Essential guidance on safety points in primary science. Your local authority adviser should have copies.
Primary Science and Literacy Links. Rosemary Feasey (1999). The Association for Science Education.	Excellent guide on how science work can feed into literacy hours and support other work in English. An essential book for the staffroom.
Primary Science and Numeracy. Rosemary Feasey and Bob Gallear (2000). The Association for Science Education.	As above – linking science work with numeracy objectives.

2. Non-fiction books, stories and poetry for children to read and use

(A) Non-fiction books on plants – for the school library

Source	Notes
The Dorling Kindersley Picturepedia of Plants (1993). Dorling Kindersley.	The usual high standard of text and pictures in Dorling Kindersley's books make this a very good purchase for the library.
Plant: Eyewitness Guides (1989). Dorling Kindersley. See also the DK website listed below in the ICT websites section.	As above and with lots of information. Produced in association with the Natural History Museum and Kew Gardens.

Source	Notes
Incredible Plants – Dorling Kindersley Inside Guides. Barbara Taylor (1997). Dorling Kindersley.	Yet another DK masterpiece. This book shows a lot of detail on plant structure and complements the other DK guides. Very good on plant feeding and insect-eating plants.
The Clue Books: Flowers. Gwen Allen and Joan Denslow (1997). Oxford University Press.	Very good guide for children and teachers to use for flower and plant identification and information.
Collins Pocket Guides: Wild Flowers. Richard Fitter, Alistair Fitter and Marjorie Blamey (1996). Harper Collins.	For the teacher and older pupils. Very good illustrations.
Mighty Microbes – Get to Know Your Germs Thompson Yardley (1993). Cassell.	Fascinating book for the library. Well illustrated with cartoon-style explanations and readable text.
Why Do Sunflowers Face the Sun? Questions Children Ask About Nature. Terry Martin (1996). Dorling Kindersley.	There are a number of questions that children ask about nature here. This could be used to stimulate children to ask their own questions and design booklets that provide information to answer them.
All Ways of Looking at Flowers. Jane Walker (1993). Gloucester Press.	Some good ideas for activities that children can use. Also provides some 'amazing facts' that will fascinate children.
Flower. Moira Batterfield (1995). Teeney Books.	Tells the story of pollination and the life cycle of plants – suitable for infants and lower juniors.
How Plants Grow. Angela Royston. (1999). Heinemann.	Part of a six-book series on 'plants'. Very clearly explained concepts and excellent illustrations. Very useful addition to the library for infants and lower juniors.

(B) Fiction

Book details	*Comments – links with plants*
The Tree House. Gillian Cross (1994). Mammoth.	Links to changes during the year, e.g. leaves grow to hide children in their tree house. Also technology link – getting the potato 'ammunition' up the tree.
James and the Giant Peach. Roald Dahl (1961). Allen and Unwin.	The classic story – often read in schools. Concepts that can follow from reading the story include: *forms* and *variety* of fruits, *sizes* of fruits and *maturation/ripening*, pips, stones and *seeds, types of animals* that feed on fruits and *dispersal.*
The Tiny Seed. Eric Carle (1987). Hodder and Stoughton.	Another classic for young children. Tells the story of a tiny seed dispersed with others. Links with seeds and conditions for growth and the life cycle of a plant.
Growing Food. Bernard Ashby and Anne Wilson (1999). Bloomsbury.	A group of residents are asked what they want to do with a derelict factory site. A family plants a seed and eventually the whole community has allotments. Excellent for opinions and issues on environment as well as values and of course growth, variety of vegetable types, etc.
Daisy and Jack in the Garden. Prue Theobalds. Uplands Books.	Daisy and Jack grow gardens on each side of a shed, Jack grows a variety of vegetables while Daisy doesn't tend her garden and she grows a variety of wild flowers. Issues are raised – shows value of natural environment.

Book details	*Comments – links with plants*
The Little Apple Tree. Inga Moore (1994). Simon and Schuster.	Lucy has mobility problems and loves to walk in the garden her dad tends. She particularly loves an old apple tree but it doesn't bear fruit. Her dad wants to remove it. She persuades him not to and she follows the life of the tree through the year until it eventually bears fruit.
Ben's Bean. Pat Moore and Tim Archbold (1995). Orchard books.	An adventure story putting a different spin on the traditional fairy tale.
The Very Hungry Caterpillar. Eric Carle (1974). Puffin Books.	You could use this classic to ask children what caterpillars like to eat – if they all eat the same type of plant, i.e. cabbage. Could be used to introduce the idea of food chains.
Fungus the Bogeyman. Raymond Briggs (1977). Puffin Books.	You can use this classic with children in many ways. The bogeymen have '*bogey* bags', which are designed to maximise decay. The book deals with a number of ideas such as *decay, decomposition, recycling* and *pollution* and is great fun.

The following tales and rhymes, which may be found in various children's collections, could also be used:

'The Enormous Turnip'	Sorting vegetables into sets. Which ones come from roots?
'Jack and the Beanstalk'	Comparing seed germination and seedling growth. Who can grow the tallest bean seedling? Do some seeds grow into bigger plants than other seeds? Etc.
'Mary, Mary Quite Contrary'	Seed germination and growth. Questions could include: Can you get these seeds to grow . . . without water . . . in soil . . . without soil . . . under water?

(C) Poetry

You will need to check collections and anthologies of children's poetry to see if you can find some of these poems – you may well know of others.

Poem	Poet	Links with plant science
Seeds	James Reeves	Descriptions of seed forms and use – good use of descriptive analogies.
Shiny	James Reeves	Descriptions of chestnut leaf before it unfurls and charming use of simile, e.g. inside of buttercup like *'burnished gold'*.
The Intruder	James Reeves	Useful link to habitats in woodland trees – also refers to disturbance of habitat and to camouflage.
Flowers and Frost	James Reeves	'Flowers and frost can never agree' – seasonal change and effects of temperature – life cycles.
The Dream of the Cabbage Caterpillars	Libby Houston	Traces the life cycle of the butterfly but crucially relates each stage to a plant e.g. eggs laid on leaves – caterpillar feeding – adult drinking nectar – 'sweet fuel from trembling bright flowers'.
Leaves	Ted Hughes	Superb example – a must – takes you through all the changes and deals with the notion of recycling and seasons in nature.
Apples	Laurie Lee	Mainly deals with animals feeding as decomposers on fallen apples – also good for names and variety of plants.
Invitation to the Bee	Charlotte Smith	Mentions many of the adaptive features of flowers that attract bees.

Poem	Poet	Links with plant science
Trees	Sara Coleridge	Lists names of trees and where they are found – good example of one-liners that children could write.
Spring	William Shakespeare	Three rhyming couplets from *Love's Labours Lost* – flowers signalling spring.
The Wood Spurge	Christina Rossetti	Poem celebrating the discovery that the spurge flower is really like 'three cups in one'.
Green Man in the Garden	Charles Causley	Describes the appearance of the mythological figure the green man – relates all his features to the plants, e.g. bones are made of elder branch.

3. ICT resources including useful websites

(A) Websites

	Notes
Website addresses www-saps.plantsci.cam.ac.uk	This is the main site for Science and Plants for Schools (SAPS) (see also the section on organisations). There are many useful links from this site to others concerned with plant science around the world. Children can ask questions about plants. There are several answers already on the database. The two links below are parts of the SAPS site that will give you instructions connected with some of the activities mentioned in this book.
www-saps.plantsci.cam.ac.uk/ worksheets/supsci1	This will give you the instructions for making an eco-column that includes growing insectivorous plants.

Website addresses	Notes
www-saps.plantsci.cam.ac.uk/ worksheets/ssheet15.html	This will give you the instructions for making a model flower from a plastic bottle and other materials.
www.namss.org.uk/fests.htm	A site providing dates of festivals and celebrations in different cultures.
www.indiatimes.com	Very good site providing inform-ation on the traditions of all the major festivals of the world religions. Search under 'Spirituality' section.
www.hindunet.org	Gives information and updates on all the Hindu events of the year.
www.eyewitness.dk.com	The Dorling Kindersley Eyewitness books are all on this site and the pages and pictures can be viewed and read on screen. Try titles shown in the books list above.
www.biology.anu.edu.au/ research-groups/Plantsc	An Australian site that provides some interesting experiments. Try measuring how strong bean seeds are.
www.ajkids.com	Good site where children can ask a question and then get directed to some useful information.
www.utopia.knoware.us/users/aart	A US website giving details and pictures of every floral family found in Europe – one of the best sites for detailed information and images.
www.bubl.ac.uk/link/p/ plantdistribution.htm	A site that will take you to a number of sources of information and images. Very useful for background and project work/ displays.

(B) Software – programmes and CD-ROMs

Software and source	Comment
My World, Available from: Granada Learning Ltd, Granada TV, Quay St Manchester M60 9EA. Tel. 0161 827 2927	The best introduction to on-screen work for science. You can get a package on 'living and growing' that deals with plants. *My World Chart* will allow pupils to record and chart growth and other measurements of plants.
Survey, Available from: SPA, PO Box 59, Tewkesbury, Gloucestershire GL20 6AB. Tel. 01684 833700.	A very good programme to introduce graphing and data handling to all ages. Especially good for infants through to Y4/5 and really a progression from *My World* and a good preparation for spreadsheet graphing. Handles a good range of plant work very well from pictographs for younger children to histograms for surveys of plant variation.
Garden Wildlife, Available from: Anglia Multimedia, Anglia House, Norwich NR1 3JG.	This CD-ROM allows children to explore garden and urban habitats and to discover facts about plants and animals that live there. This CD has a very high level of on-screen interaction and can be used from top infants to upper juniors.

4. Organisations and places to visit

Details of organisation/place	Comment on use
Science and Plants for Schools (SAPS). Head office at: Homerton College, Cambridge CB2 2PH Tel. 01223 507168. See also the website address (above).	This is the organisation dedicated to helping schools teach good plant science. They run training courses throughout the year and you can apply for a grant to help you with the cost of making light banks. The 'fast plant' technology referred to in this book comes from this organisation but they do a lot more than this. If you join SAPS they will also send you a regular newsletter called 'Osmosis' full of ideas for classroom activities.
Seed, kits and instructions for growing fast plants are available from: Philip Harris Ltd, Novara Group, Novara House, Excelsior Road, Ashby de la Zouch, Leicestershire LE65 1NG, Tel. 0870 6000193.	Philip Harris are the suppliers of materials and seeds that you need to grow 'fast plants'. All the instructions for planting and maintenance are provided with the kits.
The Shap Calendar of Religious Festivals. Available from: Shap Working Party on World Religions in Education, c/o The National Society's RE Centre, 36 Causton Street, London, SW1P 4AU. Tel. 0207 932 1194	This invaluable guide is published every year and helps teachers to plan work on festivals and celebrations into the school year. A summary of dates is also available on the Internet – see section above.

Details of organisation/place	Comment on use
BBSRC (The Biotechnology and Biological Sciences Research Council) Schools' Liaison Service, Polaris House, North Star Avenue, Swindon, Wiltshire SN2 1UH. Tel. 01793 413302.	This organisation has produced some free materials on plants for schools including a play called 'Growing pains'. There are also a number of activity sheets that you can obtain.
The Botanic Garden Education Network (BGEN), c/o The Education Officer, Birmingham Botanical Gardens, Westbourne Road, Edgbaston, Birmingham B15 3TR.	Botanic gardens are excellent places for school visits and for children to study plants. There is almost certainly one within reach of your school. This organisation will advise you on the best venues for you to use and the educational facilities they offer.

Concept summary: Summary of the ideas in this book and how they link with the National Curriculum and QCA scheme of work for science

Chapter	Key science ideas	Reference to National Curriculum programmes of study	Reference to units of the QCA scheme of work for science
1. Our world of plants	Plants are used to make many everyday objects. Plants have roots, stems and leaves and all can be eaten. The amount of rubber in a material affects its friction.	Key Stage 1: Sc2: 3b. Sc3: 1a, 1c. Key Stage 2: Sc3: 1a. Sc4: 2c.	2D: Grouping and changing materials. 3C: Characteristics of materials.
2. Variety is the spice of plant life	Variety defines the range of plant types and groups. There are many groups of plants without flowers. Individuals of one plant type vary. Variations are inherited.	Key Stage 1: Sc2: 4b. Key Stage 2: 4b, 4c.	2C: Variation. 4B: Habitats.
3. Carry on growing	Germination requires warmth, moisture and air. Growth involves the addition of new mass to the plant. There is a life cycle of development from seed to seed again.	Key Stage 1: Sc2: 1c, 3a,3b,3c. Key Stage 2: Sc2: 1b, 3a, 3c.	1B: Growing plants. 2B: Plants and animals in the local environment. 3B: Helping plants grow well.
4. Feeding the world	Plants make food using energy from the sun. All life depends on energy from plants and therefore on the sun. Leaves are designed to trap maximum light.	Key Stage 2: Sc2: 1b, 1c, 3a, 3b, 5d, 5e.	3B: Helping plants grow well. 4B: Habitats. 6A: Interdependence and adaptation.
5. Water: a question of balance	Plants take in water and nutrients from soil. Plants have a transport system to carry water and nutrients. Plants are adapted to deal with problems of water supply and loss.	Key Stage 1 : Sc2: 3a. Key Stage 2: Sc2: 3c, 5c.	3B: Helping plants grow well. 6A: Interdependence and adaptation.
6. Carrying on	Flowers are adapted to be pollinated by animals or the wind. Fruits and seeds are dispersed to new places. Plants can reproduce themselves without flowers or seeds.	Key Stage 1: Sc2: 3a, 3b, 4b. Key Stage 2: Sc2: 1b, 3d, 4b, 4c.	2B: Plants and animals in the local environment, 2C: Variation. 5B: Life cycles.
7. Plants and the environment	Habitats are characterised by the plants that live in them. The distribution of plants can vary within a habitat. Habitats change through succession. Conservation manages and preserves a range of habitat types.	Key Stage 1: Sc2: 1c, 5a, 5b, 5c. Key Stage 2: Sc2: 1c, 5a, 5b, 5c, 5d, 5e.	2B: Plants and animals in the local environment. 4B: Habitats. 6: Interdependence and adaptation. 5/6H: Enquiry in environmental and technological contexts.
8. Mighty microbes	Microbes cause decay and help recycle nutrients. Microbe action can be harmful or beneficial. Microbe action is affected by moisture and temperature.	Key Stage 2: Sc1: 1a (Edward Jenner). Sc2: 5f.	6B: Micro-organisms.
9. Celebrating with plants	Plants are used in a wide range of festivals and celebrations in all cultures. Plants have historical and cultural significance for people.	Key Stages 1 and 2: Pupils' cultural development. Key Stage 2: Developing good relationships and respecting differences between people.	

Acknowledgements

I would like to thank the following people and organisations who provided material, ideas and support for this book:

Anne Goldsworthy and *Ginn Publishing Co.* for permission to use the planning flower used on copiable worksheet 10.1.

Roy Phipps, Senior Lecturer in Science Education at Bretton Hall College of the University of Leeds for permission to use the 'flowerpot model' to show progression in plant investigations.

Tate and Lyle Sugars for permission to use a number of photographic images and the model flower idea on copiable worksheet 6.3.

Richard Price, Director, and all at *Science and Plants for Schools* (SAPS) for the inspiration and ideas on plant science and for all the work they do to make plant work accessible and exciting for teachers and children.

Susan Humphries and *Sian Gates* from the Coombes School in Berkshire for providing wonderful images of children celebrating with plants.

David Wray and *Anne Hallam*, Education Technicians at Bretton Hall College for providing many of the photographs and for their time and diligence in growing and looking after all those plants.

My wife Shân for reading through a draft version of this book to see if it made sense and for putting up with all the bits of paper and frustrations with the computer.

Appendix 1

A list of images on the CD-ROM with background information

Using the CD-ROM

There are over 200 images of plants on the CD-ROM supplied with this book. They provide resources that can be used by children and teachers in a number of different ways. You could use the CD-ROM in the following ways:

- children can select, cut and paste images of plants and plant structures into their own work;

- teachers can show images to the whole class using a computer, interactive whiteboard, TV screen or overhead projector;

- images can be included in teacher-written classroom materials, worksheets and tests;

- the CD-ROM provides a resource (if loaded onto a server, internal school network and/or website) which will be accessible to all teachers and children in the school as well as an outside audience, including parents;

- images can be set in screen savers, multimedia presentations and scrolling slide-shows;

- images can be used as sources for cross-curricular work including art and PSHE;

- use the images to stimulate discussion, by asking children what they might mean to them, what questions the images raise, or what further things they might want to know.

The list of categories and images on the CD-ROM

Some of the images are straightforward and the teacher can make use of them without any further background information, or by referring to the relevant text in this book. Notes have been provided for the images that are a little more obscure or that have interesting or unusual aspects. The images are listed in the order in which they appear on the CD-ROM.

Image folder	Image title	Notes about the image
Ancient plants	Ancient pines	*Pinsapos* pines have been growing in this part of Southern Spain for thousands of years. The ones shown on the mountainside here are about 250 years old. These forests are under threat as water is extracted from the area to support tourism and development.
	Big cedars	These are seen growing in a botanical park outside Lisbon, Portugal.
	Car driving through redwood	Redwoods are some of the world's largest plants. The car and road give an idea of scale. California, USA.
	Bristlecone pine	This is one of the oldest known plants. Some specimens are reckoned to be over 4,000 years old. Nevada, USA.
	Fallen redwood	You can get some idea of the thickness of the trunk from this picture.
	A lone *Pinsapos*	
	Redwood forest	
	Redwood house	Some of the oldest redwoods in California have even been used for houses – yet the tree above can still live.
	Redwood house: close-up	
	Roots holding up a building	The roots of this giant tree are holding up what is left of this church.
	Tall redwoods by road	
		The car gives an idea of scale.
	Yew tree in graveyard	
		Some yews are over 1,000 years old and were traditionally planted around churches to ward off evil spirits.
Celebrations	Beating the bounds	See the notes about this tradition on page 118.
	Christmas tree carrying	In this school all activities that relate to celebrations are communal events of great meaning that encourage children to co-operate and work together.
	Divali log candles	See notes about this festival on page 121.
	Easter egg basket	The children have made a sort of nest from leaves to put their painted (pace) eggs in.
	Decorated Easter eggs	
	Collecting evergreens	
	Making flower pictures	This is an example of 'ephemeral art' – art that lasts as long as the flowers. The technique was pioneered in this country by an artist called Andy Goldsworthy.
	Daffodil harvest	Daffodils are collected by children for St David's day celebrations. The children are encouraged to think about how many flowers should be picked.
	Collecting flowers for Mothers' Day	
	Palm Sunday celebrations	

Image folder	Image title	Notes about the image
	Silver birch tree rings	The children are talking about age and recycling of materials. The birch sections are used for children to display natural objects from the environment.
	St. Patrick's Day potatoes	
	Making Sukkot shelters	See notes about this festival on page 121.
	Virgin passo	During Holy Week in Seville in Southern Spain, huge wooden carved floats are carried through the streets. Some of the floats carry a beautiful statue of the Virgin Mary. The Virgin float is always decorated with white flowers like lilies and carnations.
	Spanish Holy Week: Woven palm	People in Spain decorate their houses with palms to remember when Jesus entered the holy city of Jerusalem on a donkey.
Conservation and green issues	Badlands	This is what happens if crops are grown again and again on soil without proper care. The topsoil is blown or washed away and not much will grow again.
	Green composting	The green waste from gardening can be recycled e.g. to make 'mulch' to go onto gardens or be turned into a kind of fertiliser called 'compost'.
	Green waste collection	
	Log roll	Recycling a fallen tree to make a seat on a local nature reserve. The project involves local families and children.
	Making a chipping path	Trimmed branches and dead trees can be 'chipped' to make materials for paths on the nature reserve.
	Pines damaged by acid rain	These pines are hundreds of miles away from big cities but can still be killed by chemicals that make the rain acid, and clog up and kill the leaves. Smoky Mountains, Tennessee, USA.
	Seat	An old tree trunk makes an ideal seat for people to enjoy the nature reserve.
	Trolley	People throw all sorts of rubbish into streams and ponds. The conservation volunteers will have to get it out.
	Wood path	Spreading wood chips onto the nature reserve path through the woods.
Crops and agriculture	Combine harvester	
	Corn on the cob	The seeds lie along the 'cob' in rows. Each one has come from a fertilised egg cell (ovule)
	Corn plants	You can see the whole fruit that encases the cob here.
		The corn plants can be very tall – 'as high as an elephant's eye' – as the song from *Oklahoma* put it.

Image folder	Image title	Notes about the image
	Cotton plants	Children rarely associate the cotton clothes we wear with a plant. The cotton fibres come from the protective hairs of the fruit surrounding the seeds of the plant.
	Huge prairie fields	Some of the wheat fields on the great plains of Canada and USA are many hectares in size to make harvesting more efficient.
	Apple harvest	Sometimes plants produce much more than we can possibly eat – yet so many people in the world do not have enough food.
	Mowing hay	'Silage' – a sort of food for cattle is made from hay. What plant did the hay come from?
	Prairie harvest	Point out what is happening here, and ask children what happens to the grain next and how it could end up as bread.
Desert plants	Cactus in flower	Children often think that cacti are flowerless plants.
	Desert cacti and succulents	Various shapes and sizes. The spines are modified leaves and protect the plant. The stems of cacti are green so they can make food instead of the leaves.
	Echinocactus	A ball-shaped cactus.
	Prickly pear cactus	This type of cactus came from South America and was introduced into Australia where it became a great nuisance, driving out the local desert plants.
	Cactus growing wild	Huge protective spines and a tough leathery skin can be seen. This one is growing wild near an ancient Arabian castle in Spain.
	Succulents	Like cacti, succulents grow in arid areas with low rainfall. They have small, thick leaves that contain a sort of slime that can hold onto water. Lagos, Portugal.
Dunes and marsh	Sand dune	As dune grasses like marram and other plants get established they stabilise the sand. The dunes can be up to 50 feet high. They are called *grey dunes* because if you dig down into the sand you can find that a certain amount of dead plant material (compost) has started to build up. Ardnamurchan Point, Scotland
	Purple viper's bugloss	A typical dune plant with deep roots and hairy stems and leaves adapted to cut down water loss from the plant.
	Marsh	Surprisingly, behind the grey dunes, the soil is peaty and often gets waterlogged giving marshy conditions and a home for wetland plants. Ardnamurchan Point, Scotland
	Sea Spurry	Fleshy leaves seen, which help to cut down water loss. Tavira, Portugal.
	Wet fenlands	Rushes and sedges abound here and the windmill is used as a pump to control water levels. Wickham Fen, Lincolnshire.

Image folder	Image title	Notes about the image
Flowerless plants	Bracken fern	The most common large fern of scrub, woodland and open hillsides.
	Bracket fungus	Commonly seen sprouting from tree trunks and fallen logs in woodland.
	Fern leaf: close up	
	Ferns growing on a tree	These are examples of *epiphytes* – plants that grow on others. They are not parasites however and do not harm the plant they grow on.
	Fucus seaweed	The orange-brown tips of the *fronds* (algae don't have true leaves) are fruiting bodies and these contain the plant's spores.
	Fucus seaweed:close up	This type is called *serrated wrack* – can you see why?
	Giant tree ferns: Lisbon	In the Montserrat gardens outside Lisbon is one of the world's best collections of tree ferns. These are reminders of the great *carboniferous forests* of 600 million years ago that were swamped by the sea and later formed the coal, which we now mine.
	Kelp: close up	This plant has a very tough frond and *stipe* (stalk). The giant kelps of California are the fastest growing plants on Earth.
	Lichens on trees	Healthy lichen growth is a sign of clean air – they are very sensitive to pollution.
	Mosses	There are several different types growing on this rotting log.
	Orange lichens	These are common at the seaside on cliffs, rocks, buildings and walls – well above the high-tide mark. The pink flowers are *sea pinks* and the birds are *razorbills*. Outer Hebrides, Scotland.
	Palmaria seaweed	Seaweeds are *algae* and there are red, green and brown varieties. The reds are usually found nearer the low water mark.
	Pelvetia seaweed	The common name for this seaweed is *channelled wrack* and it is only found right at the top of the shore near to the high water mark. It can roll its fronds around a channel running down the middle so that it conserves water when the tide is out.
	Tree fern	A close up of an individual example.
Flowers *Fungi*	White lily flower	A good example to show children the orange coloured *pollen sacs* of the *anthers* and the green sticky *stigma*.
	Calico flower	The scientific name of this climber from the Brazilian rainforest is *Arisotolochia elegans* but it is often referred to as the *Dutchman's pipe* for obvious reasons.
	Arum lily	A common houseplant with an unusually shaped flower. Relatives in the wild are called *Lords and Ladies*.

Image folder	Image title	Notes about the image
	Big sunflower	These flowers can turn to face the sun. You can see that the seeds are starting to show at the centre of the flower.
	Bladder campion	
	Bluebells: close up	Bluebells come into flower on the woodland floor well before the leaves of the trees have established themselves, so that they can get maximum sunlight.
	Borage	
	Bougainvillea	This plant with its striking red, purple or orange flowers is very commonly grown as a climber on Mediterranean buildings and hotels – children may see it if they go on holiday to these places.
	Yellow broom	This plant produces seeds in a pod.
	Dandelion seed head	Good for showing parachute fruits/seeds.
	Early summer flowers	The warm spring sun produces a profusion of blooms on ground that will become like semi-desert later in the year. Cramona, Seville, Southern Spain.
	Foxglove	The trumpet-shaped florets have spots to attract bees.
	Hibiscus	The Chinese shoe-flower (*Hibiscus rosa-sinensis*) is common in Mediterranean gardens. The red *stigma* can be seen held above the yellow *anthers*. This is to avoid the flower pollinating itself.
	Morning glory	It has a tube-shaped flower that attracts bees to crawl right inside towards the sweet smelling *nectar*.
	Mesembryanthemums	These brightly-coloured succulents are natives of Southern Africa, where they can exist in semi-arid places.
	Bergamot	A common flower of woodlands in the Appalachian Mountains of the USA. Smoky Mountains, Tennessee, USA.
	Pink roses	
	Plantain flowers	Note the very obvious anthers that hang right outside the flower heads. This is typical of wind-pollinated flowers.
	Poppies on waste ground	Poppies were a common sight in the cornfields. They were chosen to remind us of the cornfields of Flanders where millions of men died in the First World War.
	Tropical rainforest orchids	
	Wild flowers: Spain	
	Wood anemones	Another flower which, like the bluebell, has timed its growth and flowering to take advantage of the light of early spring.
	Wood sorrel	Can you tell the difference between the leaves of this flower and those of the wood anemone?

Image folder	Image title	Notes about the image
	Bracket fungus: red-brown	Note the colour and the growth habit of the concentric rings.
	Bracket fungus: blue-grey	
	Coprinus fungi	Note the shape of the *cap* and the *gills* that you can see on the fully opened specimen.
	Gomphidius fungi	The gills that bear the *spores* can be seen on the specimen, lying horizontally.
	Bricktop fungi	
	Leccin	
	Mould: fruiting bodies	Close-up showing the club-shaped fruiting bodies of a mould.
	Psathyrella fungi	Can you see the place where the cap was attached to the stalk?
Habitats	Weeded-up pond	This pond has been invaded by New Zealand pygmy weed (*Crassula helmsii*) another problem immigrant plant that can turn a pond into a marsh in months.
	Acacia thorn scrub	Small trees that are rather indigestible for elephants etc. Tanzania, Africa.
	Cotton grass	This plant is common on boggy, acid soils that are poor in nutrients. You can also see common *cross-leaved heather* in this photo. North Yorkshire Moors.
	Long-grass savannah	Typical long grasslands of Africa. Serengeti, Africa.
	Heather moorland	Typical upland moors where grouse commonly nest. North Yorkshire Moors.
	Savannah with woodland	You can see the edge of the famous Ngorogoro crater in the distance. Tanzania, Africa.
Insectivorous plants	Pitcher plant	Insects fall down into a watery reservoir and cannot climb up the slippery sides.
	Insectivorous plants: various	These are growing in compost that has been adjusted to mimic the nitrogen poor soils where they naturally grow.
	Model of a venus fly trap	Made by a class of Y4 children.
	Model of a pitcher plant	
	Butterwort: purple	Butterworts have sticky leaves that trap insects.
	Butterwort: pink	
	Flava coppertop	Insects fall down the very long tube-like flowers.
	Venus flytrap	Some of the leaf pairs are open, ready to be triggered if an insect touches them.

Image folder	Image title	Notes about the image
	Huntsman's horn	Sundews have leaves with rows of sticky hairs that glue the insect down when it lands on them.
	Long-leaved sundews	
	Sundew	
	White pitcher plant	
Leaf forms	Umbrella grass	Leaves arranged in a fan shape at the top of the plant.
	Dragon tree	Leaves arranged in a spiral up the stem – there are no side branches.
	Parlour palm	So-called because it was popular in Victorian households. Leaves alternate in opposite rows.
	Rainforest 'drip tips': rounded	
	Rainforest 'drip tips': pointed	
	Large rainforest leaf	Leaflets are arranged as opposite pairs.
	Downy leaves	The soft down on leaves cuts down water loss.
	Fan arrangement of leaves	
	Paired arrangement of leaves	
	Rosette arrangement of leaves	Growing points are protected at the centre of the plants and the leaves get maximum sunlight. They are very resistant to trampling on lawns and paths.
	Spiral arrangement of leaves	Each pair of leaves is set at a different angle to the one below and so on up the stem, so that all leaves can get maximum light without shading the ones below.
Parasitic plants	Yellow broomrape	Only the *spike* of flowers can be seen. The body of the plant called the *horstoria* exists underground and the plant depends on its *host* for making food.
	Dodder on a marrow plant	*Parasites* depend on their host for food, but they must be careful to take just what they need without harming the host.
	Rafflesia	This is the world's largest flower, measuring over 2m across. It is named after Sir Stamford Raffles and is common in the jungles of Malaysia.
	Spruce with mistletoe	The light green is the mistletoe. See section on Christmas plants, page 122 to find out what it represents.
Plant activities	Fast plants	Shows the plants at different ages.
	A flower model	This is an example of the model that can be made using the activity on copiable worksheet 6.3.
	Geranium kept in the dark	You can see that the stems and leaves are very thin and yellow. This is typical of an etiolated plant.

Image folder	Image title	Notes about the image
	Germination bottle	
	Moisture meters	
	Onion grown in bottle	
	Sunflower seedlings	You can see that the seed coat is still attached to the seed leaves (*cotyledons*). In this type of germination, the shoot pulls the seed up above ground and the seed is then discarded.
	Vegetative organs	A selection of examples. Children could name/label these.
Spring flowers and bulbs	Amaryllis	A good bulb to have growing in the classroom after Christmas.
	Celandine	This flower develops from underground root tubers.
	Daffodils	This is St Mary's Abbey, York in the background.
	Dwarf white rhododendrons	
	Forsythia	
	Magnolia	These ornamental trees from the Orient produce their flowers before their leaves.
	New chestnut growth	You can see the growth bursting out from the sticky buds.
	Spring meadow	
	Tulips	
	Willow in spring	
Subtropical	A locust tree	A type of acacia tree.
	Acanthus spinosus	A native of Greece. The shape of the flower *spike* is said to have inspired the design of Corinthian columns in Ancient Greece.
	Ant galls on an acacia tree	The plant produces these brown *nodules* and ants live in them. The ants get sap for food from the tree and, in turn, protect the tree by attacking any would-be grazers. An example of a plant/animal association of mutual benefit. Tanzania, Africa.
	Bird of paradise flower	Sometimes called a *crane flower*. It is a native of South Africa.
	Bottlebrush tree	Flowers named for obvious reasons.
	Bottlebrush tree: close up	The flowers are nearly all composed of very stiff stamens.

Image folder	Image title	Notes about the image
	Canary Island palm	These trees are *dioecious*, which means that individual plants are either male or female. This is a female one, bearing fruits. They come from the Canary Islands – hence the name.
	Eucalyptus tree	Often planted as ornamental trees and as crops (for oils). They use up a lot of water and cause problems if planted in arid climates. Seville, Spain.
	European fan palm	The only common palm native to Europe – most others have been imported.
	Fig tree	Showing fruits that turn purple when they are ripe.
	Mimosa	Ornamental tree shown in flower. Antequera, Spain.
	Orange tree	These are planted as ornamental trees in some Spanish cities. The fruits of these trees are bitter tasting and used to make marmalade – Seville oranges.
	Palm tree in fruit	
	Prickly pear cactus	*Optunia*. These are cultivated in Mexico and South America for their edible fruits and for the sap, which is used to make gum and candles.
	Prickly succulent	
	Red hot cat's tail bush	*Acalypha hispida*, a native of Malaya.
	Seed pods of the locust tree	
	Succulent in flower	This one is called the *Agave* or *century plant* because it was thought to flower only once every hundred years.
	Thorn apple tree	Sometimes called *angels' trumpets*. Originally from South America and often planted in Southern Europe as an ornamental tree. The seeds and sap are poisonous. Algarve, Portugal.
	Upside-down tree (monkey puzzle)	An unusually shaped tree, sometimes seen in botanical gardens and parks.
	Various palm trees	
Swamps	Alligator in duckweed	The alligator lies still, and from a distance looks almost like a floating log. The nose and body are covered in a tiny plant called *duckweed* that covers the water of the swamp. Honey Island Swamp, Louisiana, USA.
	Drowned forest: Ontario	The water table has risen as the ground has subsided and now parts of the forest are flooded. Bruce Trail, Central Ontario, Canada.
	Flooded woods: Florida	A habitat similar to that above, but this time sub-tropical and home to many snakes. Myaka Lakes, Florida, USA.

Image folder	Image title	Notes about the image
	Mangrove swamp: Florida	This sort of woodland grows along the edge of the sea in many subtropical areas and is one of the richest habitats on Earth.
	Quebec wetland	The province of Quebec in Canada contains the widest range of wetlands in the world.
	Spanish moss on trees	This moss grows on trees, hanging in the moist and warm air. Honey Island Swamp, Louisiana, USA.
	Honey Island Swamp: USA	The trees are cedars, and they can withstand rotting for many years. Honey Island Swamp, Louisiana, USA.
	Water hyacinth	This is a plant that has invaded swamps, and can strangle them as they grow into a vast mat of vegetation.
Trees	Pine woods	The ground can be very dry and sandy in some of these woods.
	A grove of maple trees	Notice how thin and tall the trees have grown in their struggle to reach the light. Perhaps this wood needs some of the trees thinning out? Bruce Trail, Central Ontario, Canada.
	Almond trees in blossom	Some of the first trees to show blossom in Spring. Roundhay Park, Leeds.
	Baobab tree	Thought by local people to have been planted upside down by the devil. It is often a source of much-needed water that is stored in its roots and stem. Tanzania, Africa.
	Bonsai tree with spiral trunk	The art of *bonsai* involves trimming roots, leaves and stems so that growth is controlled and slowed. The trunks of trees can be made to grow around wire so that various shapes result.
	Colorado blue pine	A very popular garden and park tree from the USA. You might just be able to make out the CN Tower of Toronto in the background – the world's tallest structure at over 1800 feet high (584 m).
	Horse chestnut in flower	The flower spikes are called *candles* and are usually white.
	Ornamental Japanese maple tree	Often grown for their intricate and colourful foliage. They originate from slow-growing Japanese trees from cold habtitats.
Tropical	Banana palm	Note the huge leaves.
	Big tropical leaves	The jungle is a very humid place – you can see the water vapour as droplets (mist) in this photo.
	Bromeliads in flower	These are beautiful *epiphytes* (plants that grow on other plants), common in the rainforest. They grow at all levels on the boughs of the larger rainforest trees.

Image folder	Image title	Notes about the image
	A rainforest orchid on tree	Some orchids can also grow as epiphytes.
	Palm tree	
	Begonias	The under surfaces of the leaves are red to make use of what little light falls on the rainforest floor. They are very popular as houseplants.
	Tropical rainforest plant	
	Tropical rainforest orchid	
Use of plants	Morris Minor Traveller	Here the wood (probably beech) has been used to make the frame of a car. Wood has even been used to make aircraft bodies. The Mosquito – a World War Two plane – was made from wood to make it lighter and therefore able to fly faster.
	Edible plants	
	Plant products	Examples of a range of products made from plants.
	Log cabin	Many of the early settlers to America made use of the local materials for their dwellings. Smokey Mountains National Park, Tennessee, USA.
Woodlands	Birchwood with bluebells	The canopy of leaves is fairly open in this type of wood allowing more grasses, shrubs and flowers to grow on the woodland floor.
	Open wood	This woodland will also allow plenty of light to fall on to lower layers, as the trees are spread out.
	Pine woods	Here the canopy of leaves is dense and the pine needles produce an acid, rather poor soil. Not much will grow under these trees.
	Pink rhododendron	These plants are native of Asia (India) but when introduced to the UK they have grown rampant in some woodlands. They do not support much insect life and this can result in a rather poor habitat.

Appendix 2

Instructions for using the CD-ROM

The purpose of the CD-ROM is to allow the user to browse and extract single images contained in the book, Primary Plants for use in other projects and presentations.

System requirements:
Questions Publishing Limited recommends the following as minimum requirements for using the CD-ROM.
- Pentium II-based PC
- 32 megabytes of system memory
- 24 x speed CD-ROM
- 640 x 480 monitor with 16 bit colour.
- Windows 95 (OSR2), Windows 98, 2000 or ME operating system.

Operating instructions:
- After inserting the disc, use windows explorer to locate the file 'start' or 'start.exe' within the CD-ROM.
- Double clicking on this icon will start the browser. Due to the high graphics content of this CD it will take a few seconds to load the first stage.
- Click on the 'next' button to move into the CD-ROM.
- Instructions are given under the heading 'Using the CD-ROM'.
- To access the pictures, click on 'Picture Menu' button. This will give you a list of all the images available.
- If your PC has problems in opening the paint program or you wish to open the picture in your own viewer, you can exit the browser and explore the CD-ROM in windows, all the pictures are located within the 'images' folder.
- The browser can be left at any time by clicking the 'exit' button or pressing ESC on the keyboard.